TABLE OF CONTENTS

INTRO

Welcome to Skylands! Our official guide to *Skylanders Spyro's Adventure* gives you everything you need to get through all 22 chapters of this clever and surprisingly sophisticated game, plus a bit more (including maps for the four Adventure Pack levels). Our comprehensive story walkthrough uses a detailed overhead map to guide you through each chapter.

Our screenshots are particularly helpful because Activision granted us access to the in-game "camera." This let us move the view angle to give you a better idea of what you face. For example, we provide wide-angle overhead shots of some of the more difficult movement puzzles. Sure, it's close to cheating but hey, that's what a good guide does! This special camera access also gave us the ability to snap some really cool close-ups of the friends, foes, architecture and landscapes that you encounter in Skylands. They're also a big help when it comes to solving the puzzles you'll encounter during the adventure.

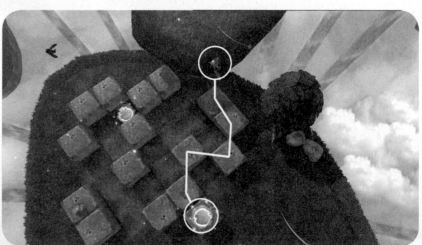

Of course, you won't need our guidance every step of the way. Much of the game is self-evident in the way that really well designed games always are. The first missions ease you into gameplay in a tutorial style that's educational and yet plenty of fun. Soon enough, however, the enemies get tougher and the puzzles more perplexing. That's when you can turn to us for help

GAME BASICS

STATS

Every Skylander has a basic set of stats that you can see when you open the Champion Details window.

♥	**MAX HEALTH**	This is the maximum number of hit points (HP) your character can have.
⚡	**SPEED**	This measures how fast your character moves.
🛡	**ARMOR**	This measures your ability to block damage from incoming enemy strikes.
⊕	**CRITICAL HIT**	This is your ability to land special blows that inflict extra damage to your target.
◎	**ELEMENTAL POWER**	This measures the extra power you gain whenever your character enters a zone strong in his/her element.
🏆	**HEROICS**	Number of Heroic Challenges you've completed.
🖥	**HERO LEVEL**	Your heroic progress on the Skylanders Spyro's Adventure website.

As you progress through the game and level up, these stats all increase. You can also boost individual stats by wearing a hat (see the following section on Hats) or completing one of Cali's heroic challenges.

ELEMENTAL ZONES

Every chapter's main location (e.g., Oilspill Island, Treetop Terrace, Molekin Mine, etc) is divided into a number of smaller zones. Each zone's name pops up onscreen whenever you enter it. Most zones are strong in just one of the elements: Magic, Water, Tech, Fire, Air, Earth, Life, or Undead. If you switch to a Skylander of that same element, his overall statistical strength increases in that zone.

LEVELING UP

Whenever you defeat an enemy, the fallen creature dissipates into tiny colored orbs that your Skylander absorbs upon approach. These increase your character's experience (XP) rating, shown on the yellow bar underneath your health gauge. When the yellow XP bar fills up your Skylander will "level up" (increase one level), all the way to level 10.

Each level-up increase boosts that particular character's stats, heals him/her completely, and triggers a powerful energy surge that slams any nearby foes with a mighty wall of damage. Gaining XP to level up is a good reason to engage every enemy you can find in each new area. It's also a good reason to replay chapters you already completed, because all the chapter's enemies respawn when you replay it.

BUFFING UP
PERSEPHONE'S UPGRADES

Every Skylander comes with a pair of powers that you can use right away. For example, Spyro starts out with his basic Flameball and Charge attacks. Later in the game you can upgrade these powers or sometimes buy entirely new ones—Spyro can gain the ability to fly, for example.

During Chapter 3: Sky Schooner Docks you meet a genial fairy named Persephone who subsequently opens a vendor shop at a podium in "The Ruins." Between missions, you can visit Persephone to buy upgrades that increase your Skylander's current powers or even add new ones. See her whenever you've accumulated enough gold and then buff up your skills. (For much more on upgrades, check out the "Meet the Skylanders" chapter.)

CALI'S HEROIC CHALLENGES

During Chapter 2: Perilous Pastures you meet Cali, a cute but tough feline gal who knows a lot about combat. Once Chapter 2 ends, she's always available for training sessions at the Ruins between main story chapters. These sessions are quick missions on a timer—you must complete a series of objectives quickly, before the clock counts down to zero. There's more information on these challenges at the end of this section of the guide, including which stats are increased after completing each one.

SPECIAL ITEMS
LOOT

Loot is everywhere in Skylands. Every barrel, bottle, box, crate, cart, cabinet, hay bale, wheelbarrow, pot, vase can possibly hold something to collect and turn into cash. To get the loot stashed inside these various objects you must smash them to smithereens first.

So here's a strategy for you: Smash everything you can smash. Often the reward for careful exploration is meager; you might smash through debris and uncover coins or gems worth just 1 or 2 gold. But sometimes you uncover a gem or other item worth 25 or 50 or even more gold. It makes thorough exploration thoroughly worth it when you hit one of these jackpots!

FOOD

Aside from leveling up, the easiest way to restore your Skylander's health is to gobble up any of the food items you find spinning in Skylands: pizza, cake, turkey legs, etc. These munchies give you varying amounts of hit points (HP), the numerical measure of each character's health. Keep in mind that your Skylanders have a "Max Health" number—that is, an upper limit on the amount of HP for that character. So if your health is good, consider bypassing food, leaving it for later.

Here's a simple example: assume your Skylander's Max Health is 300 and current health is at 290. You explore a room and find a delicious slice of pizza worth +100 HP. If you eat it now, your total HP won't go above 300, so you've only gained 10 HP. You can't store the extra 40 points—they just disappear, gone forever. So you might be better off leaving the pizza where it is. In the next room you may face a horde of Chompies who get in enough bites to lower your health to 250 or below. Now you can backtrack, eat that pizza, and get its full 50-point health benefit.

It's good to know that eating pizza can be really good for your health, isn't it?

COLLECTIBLES

SOUL GEMS

Every chapter of the game has at least one of these gorgeous purple gems somewhere in the level. Acquiring them earns you no money, no health, and no experience but Soul Gems are most definitely a "power-up" item! The reason: Each Soul Gem unlocks a very powerful upgrade, making it available for purchase from Persephone back at the Ruins.

An example is the Soul Gem you can find in the Treetop Terrace. It unlocks the powerful Anchor Cannon ability for Gill Grunt. It's not cheap—Persephone sells Anchor Cannon for 4000 gold (less any discounts earned through the collection of Winged Sapphires)—but it's worth it when you can afford it. You need powerful weapons to survive some of your encounters with Kaos and his nasty minions.

LEGENDARY TREASURES

Each chapter of the game has a single legendary treasure hidden somewhere. These special collectibles are never easy to find—in fact, they're sometimes so cleverly hidden that even a Skylander might need help tracking them down. Don't worry, though—the maps in the guide show you where each one is located, and the walkthrough tells you exactly how to solve the tricky puzzles that sometimes stand in the way.

STORY SCROLLS

Every chapter of the game also has a Story Scroll stashed somewhere in the area. These are usually easier to find than the other collectible treasures. Each scroll gives you a bit of Skylands flavor and deepens the story. Some provide useful information; others are just whimsical and fun.

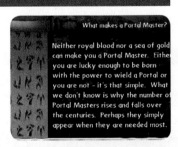

TREASURE CHESTS

Every chapter of *Skylanders Spyro's Adventure* has three Treasure Chests distributed around the level. As with hatboxes, you shake them open. Then you can scoop up the goodies that spill out: gold, gems, and other items that boost your bank account.

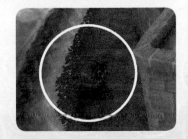

HATS

Make it a point to hunt down the hatboxes in each chapter of the game. When you find one, "shake" it open and check out the fashionable headgear inside. These hats aren't just for show: Every one gives you some kind of stat boost (increased Armor, Speed, etc) when worn. Note that your current Skylander can wear any hat you've found, any time you want even if a different Skylander found the hat.

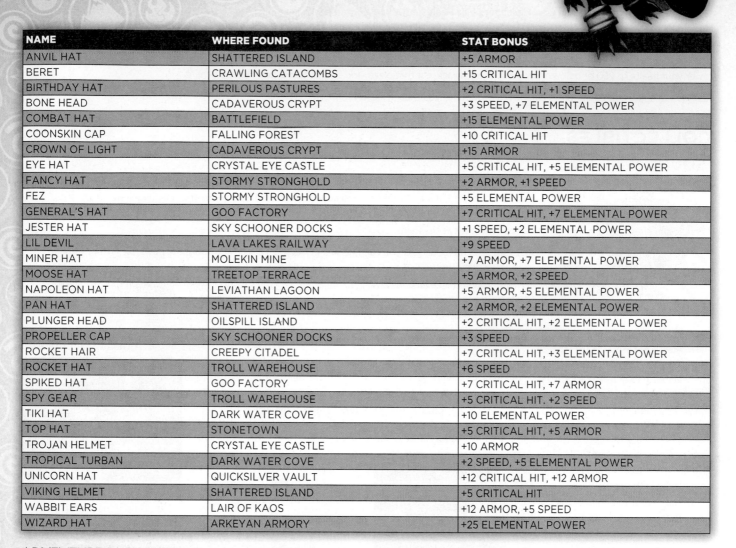

NAME	WHERE FOUND	STAT BONUS
ANVIL HAT	SHATTERED ISLAND	+5 ARMOR
BERET	CRAWLING CATACOMBS	+15 CRITICAL HIT
BIRTHDAY HAT	PERILOUS PASTURES	+2 CRITICAL HIT, +1 SPEED
BONE HEAD	CADAVEROUS CRYPT	+3 SPEED, +7 ELEMENTAL POWER
COMBAT HAT	BATTLEFIELD	+15 ELEMENTAL POWER
COONSKIN CAP	FALLING FOREST	+10 CRITICAL HIT
CROWN OF LIGHT	CADAVEROUS CRYPT	+15 ARMOR
EYE HAT	CRYSTAL EYE CASTLE	+5 CRITICAL HIT, +5 ELEMENTAL POWER
FANCY HAT	STORMY STRONGHOLD	+2 ARMOR, +1 SPEED
FEZ	STORMY STRONGHOLD	+5 ELEMENTAL POWER
GENERAL'S HAT	GOO FACTORY	+7 CRITICAL HIT, +7 ELEMENTAL POWER
JESTER HAT	SKY SCHOONER DOCKS	+1 SPEED, +2 ELEMENTAL POWER
LIL DEVIL	LAVA LAKES RAILWAY	+9 SPEED
MINER HAT	MOLEKIN MINE	+7 ARMOR, +7 ELEMENTAL POWER
MOOSE HAT	TREETOP TERRACE	+5 ARMOR, +2 SPEED
NAPOLEON HAT	LEVIATHAN LAGOON	+5 ARMOR, +5 ELEMENTAL POWER
PAN HAT	SHATTERED ISLAND	+2 ARMOR, +2 ELEMENTAL POWER
PLUNGER HEAD	OILSPILL ISLAND	+2 CRITICAL HIT, +2 ELEMENTAL POWER
PROPELLER CAP	SKY SCHOONER DOCKS	+3 SPEED
ROCKET HAIR	CREEPY CITADEL	+7 CRITICAL HIT, +3 ELEMENTAL POWER
ROCKET HAT	TROLL WAREHOUSE	+6 SPEED
SPIKED HAT	GOO FACTORY	+7 CRITICAL HIT, +7 ARMOR
SPY GEAR	TROLL WAREHOUSE	+5 CRITICAL HIT. +2 SPEED
TIKI HAT	DARK WATER COVE	+10 ELEMENTAL POWER
TOP HAT	STONETOWN	+5 CRITICAL HIT, +5 ARMOR
TROJAN HELMET	CRYSTAL EYE CASTLE	+10 ARMOR
TROPICAL TURBAN	DARK WATER COVE	+2 SPEED, +5 ELEMENTAL POWER
UNICORN HAT	QUICKSILVER VAULT	+12 CRITICAL HIT, +12 ARMOR
VIKING HELMET	SHATTERED ISLAND	+5 CRITICAL HIT
WABBIT EARS	LAIR OF KAOS	+12 ARMOR, +5 SPEED
WIZARD HAT	ARKEYAN ARMORY	+25 ELEMENTAL POWER

ADVENTURE PACK HATS

NAME	WHERE FOUND	STAT BONUS
CHEF HAT	DARKLIGHT CRYPT	+10 CRITICAL HIT, +10 ELEMENTAL POWER
PIRATE DOO RAG	PIRATE SEAS	+4 SPEED
PIRATE HAT	PIRATE SEAS	+20 CRITICAL HIT
PUMPKIN HAT	DARKLIGHT CRYPT	+10 ARMOR
ROYAL CROWN	DRAGON'S PEAK	+10 CRITICAL HIT
SANTA HAT	EMPIRE OF ICE	+20 ARMOR
WINGED HAT	DRAGON'S PEAK	+12 SPEED

CONSOLE-SPECIFIC HATS

NAME	WHERE FOUND	STAT BONUS
BOWLER HAT (PC/MAC)	PERILOUS PASTURES	+2 CRITICAL HIT, +2 ARMOR
COWBOY HAT (XBOX 360)	PERILOUS PASTURES	+2 CRITICAL HIT, +2 ARMOR
STRAW HAT (PLAYSTATION 3)	PERILOUS PASTURES	+2 CRITICAL HIT, +2 ARMOR
HAPPY BIRTHDAY! (NINTENDO WII)	PERILOUS PASTURES	+2 CRITICAL HIT, +2 ARMOR

WINGED SAPPHIRE SUMMARY

Winged Sapphires are floating blue gems you find scattered around The Ruins. For each Winged Sapphire you collect, Persophone gives a discount on her prices. The location of each Winged Sapphire is covered in the following walkthrough sections, but a summary of their locations is also provided here.

The first Winged Sapphire becomes available after you clear Oilspill Island. It's located next the spot where Persephone sells upgrades.

There are four Winged Sapphires to collect at the Ruins after clearing Creepy Citadel. The first is behind the entrance to the tracks. For the next two, you must run bombs from the beach up to the area near the engine. Throw one bomb at the rock-covered door and the other at the geyser. For the final Winged Sapphire, take the oil can from the beach and oil the train engine.

After completing Leviathan Lagoon, there's one Winged Sapphire on the path down to the beach. To get another Winged Sapphire, take the oil can to the metal man sitting on the beach. To get the fourth Winged Sapphire, take a Skylander who can cross water off the eastern edge of the beach. Use the bounce pads there to jump up to the Winged Sapphire.

When you're back at the Ruins after running through Treetop Terrace, attack the rock near Hugo and Arbo.

The final Winged Sapphire appears behind the Lock Puzzle door at the docks once you wrap up events in the Arkeyan Armory.

ACCOLADES

Accolades are achievements that you can earn as a Portal Master. The following table lists the accolades and how each is earned.

1 2 3 4 5 6 7

8 9 10 11 12 13 14

15 16 17 18 19

ACCOLADE	CONDITIONS TO EARN ACCOLADE
1 CAPTAIN	REQUIRES AT LEAST 1 NON-STARTER PACK SKYLANDER IN YOUR COLLECTION.
2 AMBASSADOR	REQUIRES 1 SKYLANDER OF EACH ELEMENT IN YOUR COLLECTION
3 SERGEANT MAJOR	REQUIRES AT LEAST 8 DIFFERENT SKYLANDERS IN YOUR COLLECTION.
4 COMMANDER	REQUIRES AT LEAST 12 DIFFERENT SKYLANDERS IN YOUR COLLECTION.
5 GENERAL	REQUIRES AT LEAST 16 DIFFERENT SKYLANDERS IN YOUR COLLECTION.
6 FIELD MARSHALL	REQUIRES AT LEAST 24 DIFFERENT SKYLANDERS IN YOUR COLLECTION.
7 MASTER OF SKYLAND	REQUIRES ALL 32 SKYLANDERS IN YOUR COLLECTION.
8 STUDENT OF THOUGHT	AT LEAST 10 STORY SCROLLS COLLECTED.
9 CHIEF SCHOLAR	REQUIRES YOU FIND ALL THE STORY SCROLLS HIDDEN THROUGH SKYLANDS.
10 SEEKER ADEPT	REQUIRES COLLECTION OF AT LEAST 10 LEGENDARY TREASURES.
11 TREASURE HUNTER	REQUIRES COLLECTION OF ALL 26 LEGENDARY TREASURES IN THE GAME.
12 POWER EXCAVATOR	REQUIRES COLLECTION OF THE SOUL GEMS FOR EACH OF THE 3 STARTER PACK SKYLANDERS.
13 SOUL WARDEN	REQUIRES COLLECTION OF ALL 32 SKYLANDERS' SOUL GEMS.
14 FASHION ELITE	REQUIRES COLLECTION OF AT LEAST 10 HATS.
15 WARDROBE SAINT	REQUIRES COLLECTION OF ALL HATS IN THE GAME.
16 ELITE AGENT	REQUIRES 1 SKYLANDER TO COMPLETE ALL 32 HEROIC CHALLENGES.
17 SAVIOR OF SKYLANDS	REQUIRES YOU TO COMPLETE THE SKYLAND ADVENTURE MODE BY RESTORING THE CORE OF LIGHT AND DEFEATING KAOS.
18 SKYLANDER SUPERSTAR	REQUIRES EARNING A 3-STAR RANKING ON ALL SKYLANDER ADVENTURE CHAPTERS.
19 GRAND ADMIRAL	REQUIRES EARNING ALL PORTAL MASTER ACCOLADES.

BATTLE MODE

Battle Mode gives you the chance to send your Skylanders to battle the Skylanders of another Portal Master! There are three Battle Mode types (Arena Rumble, Sky Goals, and SkyGem Master) and four Arenas (Cyclops Square, Mushroom Groves, Aqueduct, and Troll Factory) available initially.

Before any match begins, you are given a preview of the arena, including teleport pads, arena hazard activators, any hazards that aren't specific to the arena (such as the rocket hat and the comet).

MATCH SETTINGS

Before you launch into your Battle Mode contest, take a look at the Match Setting options available to you. Fair Fight is the option that has the biggest impact on your Battle Mode matches. The other four options impact both players equally, but Fair Fight works against people who have leveled up their Skylanders when they square off against lower level opponents. Fair Fight should be set to Yes unless you wish to give one participant an advantage.

OPTION	IF SET TO 'YES'
RESTORE HEALTH	RESTORES HP TO THE VICTOR AFTER EVERY MATCH.
POWERUPS	POWERUPS ARE AVAILABLE IN THE ARENA
FOOD	FOOD IS AVAILABLE IN THE ARENA
ARENA HAZARDS	HAZARDS ENABLED IN THE ARENA
FAIR FIGHT	EVENS OUT A FIGHT BETWEEN SKYLANDERS WHO ARE OF DIFFERENT EXPERIENCE LEVEL.

BATTLE MODE TYPES

ARENA RUMBLE

The goal of Arena Rumble is to reduce your opponent's health to 0.

SKY GOALS

Grab the electric football and carry it through the goal posts to score 7 points, or throw the ball in the goal to score 3 points. Damage your opponent to force them to drop the ball.

SKYGEM MASTER

Collect five gems before your opponent to win SkyGem Master. A single gem falls from the sky at regular intervals. If you deal enough damage to your opponent, they will drop some of their gems. Once they're on the ground, any Skylander can collect them.

BATTLE MODE: TIPS FROM THE TESTERS

The Skylanders testers were kind enough to provide some of their favorite tips for Battle Mode play. These are the folks who've been hammering away at *Skylanders Spyro's Adventure* for many, many months and understand its gameplay better than anybody.

Here's the awesome list they graciously provided:

- Recognize when an encounter is futile, i.e., going against you. In these cases go into defense mode—avoid direct confrontation if possible until you can use power-ups or any level-specific hazards/mechanics to turn the tide.

- Learn where and what power-ups spawn in each level.

- There a few hazards which certain Skylanders are immune to based on elemental affinities: Water Skylanders are immune to the rising fluid in the Aqueduct, and Fire Skylanders are immune to the rising lava in Burning Aqueduct.

- Understand the usefulness of "lobbers" vs. Skylanders with normal ranged attacks. Lobbers can fire over cover pieces or obstacles depending on height and the positioning of the lobber.

- Running away can be a powerful offensive tactic for some Skylanders! For example, Flameslinger leaves a swath of fire in his wake. An upgrade for Double Trouble allows him to cast his explosive minions while on the run, so he can flee and leave a trail of these behind him.

- Some melee/close range minions get powerful ranged attacks when fully upgraded. Among the most impressive of these is the fully upgraded Stump Smash if you choose the "Nut Master" upgrade path.

BATTLE MODE ARENAS

CYCLOPS SQUARE

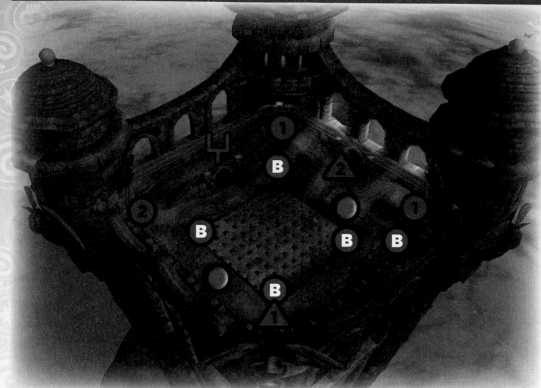

ENVIRONMENT

Cyclops Square has 5 Bounce Pads and 3 Teleporters. The north and east Teleporter send Skylanders to the South end of the courtyard. The western Teleporter leads to the northeast side.

HAZARDS

The bottom floor of Cyclops Square is rigged with spears that thrust upward when activated. Skylanders caught on the hole-filled floor when the spears appear takes damage.

MUSHROOM GROVE

ENVIRONMENT

Mushroom Grove includes 3 Bounce Pads and 2 Teleporters. Both Teleporters are on the lowest level and both lead to the same spot on the highest level. When you play Skygoals, the Teleporters are removed since the Goal takes the place of their destination.

HAZARDS

Mushroom Grove's only hazard is your opponent's Skylander!

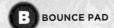 **BOUNCE PAD**  **HAZARD ACTIVATORS**   **SKYGOALS GOAL**  **TELEPORTER**  **TELEPORTER DESTINATION**

AQUEDUCT

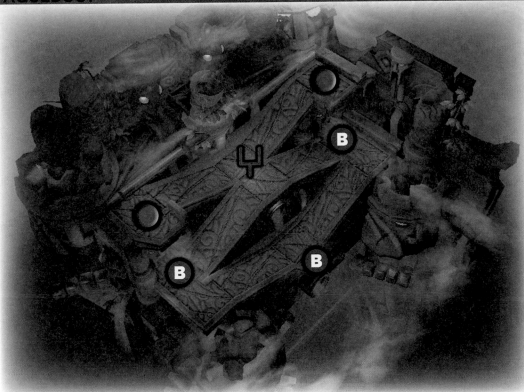

ENVIRONMENT

Aqueduct has 3 Bounce Pads but no Teleporters.

HAZARDS

The Aqueduct fills with water when either of the 2 Hazard Activators are activated. Most Skylanders caught in the water as it rises will lose health, but Water Skylanders are safe.

TROLL FACTORY

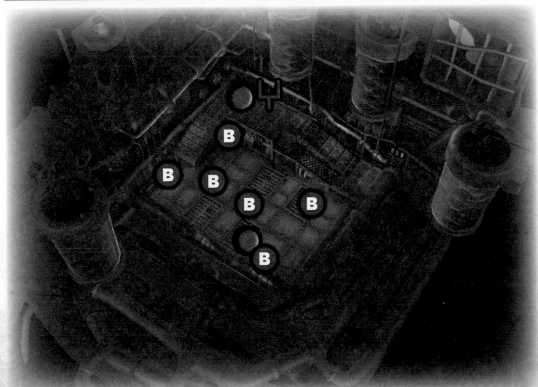

ENVIRONMENT

The Troll Factory has 6 Bounce Pads, but lacks Teleporters. There are two active conveyor belts. These belts travel toward the topmost area, making it impossible to run back down.

HAZARDS

There are two flame jets, each activated by different Hazard Activators. Most Skylanders caught in the blasts suffer damage, meaning Fire Skylanders have a slight advantage here.

UNLOCKABLE BATTLE MODE ARENAS

CUBE DUNGEON

ENVIRONMENT

Unlocked with the Dragon's Peak Adventure Pack, Cube Dungeon has 6 Bounce Pads and 3 Teleporters. The Teleporters share the same destination point on the lower floor of the dungeon.

HAZARDS

This Battle Mode Arena is named for its hazard, the Cube. The Cube bounces around the lower level, changing directions randomly. Skylanders struck by the Cube lose 20 health instantly.

ICICLE ISLE

ENVIRONMENT

Icicle Isle is unlocked with the Empire of Ice Adventure Pack. There are 5 Bounce Pads and 2 Teleporters found in this level. Both Teleporters send Skylanders to the same destination in the middle of the map.

HAZARDS

Icicle Isle does not include any damaging hazards, however the frozen areas of the level are slick. Skylanders won't respond to changes in direction very well.

B BOUNCE PAD   HAZARD ACTIVATORS   SKYGOALS GOAL  TELEPORTER  TELEPORTER DESTINATION

THE NECROPOLIS

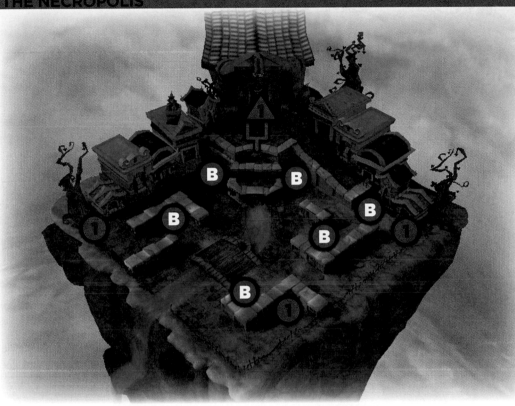

ENVIRONMENT

The Necropolis is unlocked with the Darklight Crypts Adventure Pack. This Battle Mode Arena has 6 Bounce Pads and 4 Teleporters. Each Teleporter sends Skylanders to the bridge in the center of the map.

HAZARDS

There is a cannon on the bridge in the center of the map. The cannon fires at a fixed point (you can't aim it) on the upper level of the Battle Mode Arena, near the north Teleporter. It's the same location as the goal posts in Sky Goals.

PIRATE GROTTO

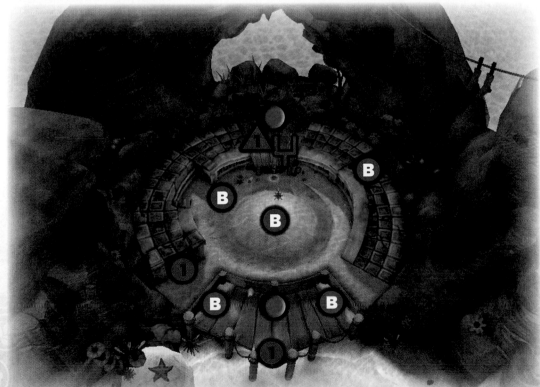

ENVIRONMENT

Pirate Grotto becomes available with the Pirate Seas Adventure Pack. There are 5 Bounce Pads and 2 Teleporters. Both Teleporters send Skylanders to the north edge of the map, near the Hazard Activator.

HAZARDS

There are two Hazard Activators, one at the north end of the map and the other at the sound, which call for naval bombardment when activated. Watch for yellow crosshairs on the ground and get out of the way of the incoming fire.

HEROIC CHALLENGES

After rescuing Cali in the Perilous Pastures, visit her in the Ruins to try the Heroic Challenges she offers. Each Skylander unlocks one Heroic Challenge, but you can use any Skylander when trying to complete a Heroic Challenge. Successful completion of a Heroic Challenge rewards the Skylander you used with a statistical bonus.

#	NAME	CHALLENGE	TIME LIMIT	REWARD	UNLOCKED WITH	
1	CHOMPY CHOMP-DOWN	HEAD FOR THE MINES AND TAKE OUT 100 ENEMIES.	2:30	ELEMENTAL POWER	WARNADO	
2	THIS BOMB'S FOR YOU	FIGHT TROLLS TO FIND THE 5 SINGING GEMS	4:00	ARMOR	GHOST ROASTER	
3	JUMP FOR IT!	JUMP AROUND AND COLLECT 75 CHARMS.	2:30	SPEED	WRECKING BALL	
4	WHERE ART THOU, PAINTINGS?	DESTROY THE 6 GHOSTLY PAINTINGS	3:00	CRITICAL HIT	SPYRO	
5	LAIR OF THE GIANT SPIDER	CLEAR THIS MINE OF 6 GIANT SPIDERS.	3:00	CRITICAL HIT	PRISM BREAK	
6	FIGHT, TELEPORT, FIGHT SOME MORE!	FIGHT AND TELEPORT YOUR WAY TO THE TRIBAL MASK.	2:30	ARMOR	LIGHTNING ROD	
7	THE THREE TELEPORTERS	FIND THE CORRECT PATH TO THE GOLDEN SPARK	3:00	ARMOR	HEX	
8	STOP, SHEEP THIEVES!	RESCUE 6 SHEEP FROM THIEVES INSIDE THE MINE.	2:30	ARMOR	DINORANG	
9	MINING FOR CHARMS	FIND MAGICAL ORE BURIED WITHIN THE ROCKS.	3:00	CRITICAL HIT	BASH	
10	DUNGEONESS CREEPS	SEARCH THE DUNGEON FOR AMBER MEDALLIONS.	3:00	CRITICAL HIT	CYNDER	
11	MINING IS THE KEY	BREAK ROCKS TO FIND THE KEYS TO FIND THE TREASURE.	4:00	SPEED	IGNITOR	
12	MISSION ACHOMPLISHED	PICK A PATH AND TAKE OUT THE CHOMPIES.	2:00	ARMOR	STUMP SMASH	

#	NAME	CHALLENGE	TIME LIMIT	REWARD	UNLOCKED WITH	
13	POD GAUNTLET	FIND YOUR WAY THROUGH THE POD MAZE.	4:30	ELEMENTAL POWER	CHOP CHOP	
14	TIME'S A-WASTIN'	TAKE OUT ENEMIES FOR EXTRA TIME NEEDED TO EXIT.	0:20	CRITICAL HIT	SONIC BOOM	
15	SAVE THE PURPLE CHOMPIES!	HIT GREEN CHOMPIES, NOT PURPLE! WARNING: THIS IS TOUGH!	2:30	ARMOR	DROBOT	
16	SPAWNER CAVE	TAKE OUT 100 CHOMPIES BY FINDING THE BEST SPAWNERS	2:00	CRITICAL HIT	TERRAFIN	
17	ARACHNID ANTECHAMBER	DEFEAT 8 GIANT SPIDERS IN THIS DUNGEON.	3:00	ARMOR	SUNBURN	
18	HOBSON'S CHOICE	FIGHT AND TELEPORT YOUR WAY TO FIND THE ANTIQUE VANITY.	3:00	SPEED	TRIGGER HAPPY	
19	ISLE OF THE AUTOMATONS	DESTROY AUTOMATONS AND OTHER ENEMIES TO SCORE 75 POINTS.	2:30	ELEMENTAL POWER	ERUPTOR	
20	YOU BREAK IT, YOU BUY IT!	HIT TROLLS, NOT PAINTINGS. WARNING: THIS IS TOUGH!	3:30	SPEED	DOUBLE TROUBLE	
21	MINEFIELD MISHAP	MAKE IT THROUGH THE MINEFIELD. WARNING: THIS IS TOUGH!	2:00	SPEED	STEALTH ELF	
22	LOBS O' FUN	EARN A TASTY TREAT BY TAKING OUT PIRATES.	3:00	CRITICAL HIT	WHIRLWIND	
23	SPELL PUNKED!	RETRIEVE THE ANCIENT BOOK OF MAGIC FROM THE SPELL PUNKS.	4:00	ARMOR	VOODOOD	
24	CHARM HUNT	HEAD FOR THE ISLANDS AND COLLECT 75 CHARMS.	3:00	CRITICAL HIT	WHAM-SHELL	
25	FLIP THE SCRIPT	CHOOSE THE RIGHT PATH TO FIND THE LOG OF NORT	5:00	ARMOR	CAMO	
26	YOU'VE STOLEN MY HEARTS!	STOP THIEVES FROM STEALING THE JEWEL HEARTS.	4:30	CRITICAL HIT	ZOOK	
27	BOMBS TO THE WALLS	USE BOMBS TO FIND 25 MAGIC CHARMS.	3:30	ELEMENTAL POWER	FLAMESLINGER	
28	OPERATION: SHEEP FREEDOM	RESCUE ALL THE SHEEP FROM THEIR TROLL CAPTORS.	3:30	CRITICAL HIT	BOOMER	
29	JAILBREAK!	RESCUE 6 MABU FROM THE CYCLOPES ISLANDS.	3:00	ARMOR	GILL GRUNT	
30	ENVIRONMENTALLY UNFRIENDLY	BLAST 7 OF THE TROLL'S PIPES.	2:30	ELEMENTAL POWER	DRILL SERGEANT	
31	CHEMICAL CLEANUP	SCORE POINTS BY DESTROYING BARRELS OF THE RIGHT COLOR.	3:30	ELEMENTAL POWER	SLAM BAM	
32	BREAK THE CATS	DESTROY THE CAT STATUES. WARNING: THIS IS TOUGH!	4:00	ARMOR	ZAP	

MEET THE SKYLANDERS

Every Skylander starts with two fundamental powers—a primary power and a secondary power. Spyro, for example, arrives in Skylands with his Flameball and Charge abilities ready to use. During Chapter 3: Sky Schooner Docks you meet Persephone, a pleasant and enterprising fairy who sets up shop at the Ruins. She's extremely happy to sell you upgrades that increase your current powers or even add new ones!

The first four upgrades are available for purchase as soon as your character can meet Persephone, and they always cost the same regardless of character: 500, 700, 900 or 1200 gold. These are your *Basic Upgrades.*

"CHOOSE YOUR PATH" UPGRADES

Once you purchase all four Basic Upgrades for your character, Persephone offers a choice between two types of upgrade paths. Typically, one focuses on improving your primary power and the other focuses on the secondary power. These are known as the *"Choose Your Path"* Upgrades.

You can choose only one of the two paths shown. Once you select a path, the upgrades in the other path are no longer available unless you Reset your Skylander, which eliminates all previously acquired upgrades, money, names, and heroic challenge buffs, and also wipes out all experience (i.e., all level advancement). In other words, you must start from scratch in order to go down the other upgrade path.

Finally, you can also buy a Super Upgrade for 4000. This choice appears in Persephone's purchase window right away, but you can't buy the Super Upgrade until you also collect a specific Soul Gem.

WINGED SAPPHIRES

Keep an eye out for the beautiful blue butterflies that flitter about in the Ruins area between story missions. These creatures are the Winged Sapphires, and every one you capture knocks two percent off the cost of upgrades. You can find a total of ten Winged Sapphires over the course of the game. Look everywhere! One even appears in the prison cell at the docks—you must solve a Lock Puzzle to get to it.

DARK SPYRO

Spyro is a rare magical dragon with the ability to harness the power of the other elements, though he prefers to master fire. However, this innate power also leaves him vulnerable to the influence of dark magic. When the Darkness is nearby, Spyro can channel its energy and combine its power with his own, becoming Dark Spyro. Over the years, he has learned to focus and control his power, using this dark magic to fight the forces of evil.

STARTING STATS

♥	MAX HEALTH	280
⚡	SPEED	50
♥	ARMOR	18
⊕	CRITICAL HIT	30
◎	ELEMENTAL POWER	46

STARTING POWERS

FLAMEBALL

PRIMARY POWER
Spyro breathes balls of flame from his mouth, incinerating enemies.

CHARGE

SECONDARY POWER
Spyro runs head down knocking over enemies with his horns.

BASIC UPGRADES

LONG RANGE RAZE

500

Enhancing Spyro's lung capacity, this ability lets Spyro shoot flameballs that travel much farther than before.

SPYRO'S FLIGHT

700

Spyro takes to the skies. Well, off the ground at least! Fly over water and move at great speed.

SPRINT CHARGE

900

Fitness counts. Spyro is able to charge for a longer distance with this upgrade.

TRIPLE FLAMEBALLS

1200

Shoot 3 Flameballs instead of one.

SUPER UPGRADE
SPYRO'S EARTH POUND

4000

Perform a devastating dive-bomb head smash while flying, damaging enemies all around you. This upgrade requires collection of the Soul Gem in Chapter 15, Crawling Catacombs.

"CHOOSE YOUR PATH" UPGRADES

SHEEP BURNER SPYRO
This upgrade path lets you further develop your Flameball attacks.

FIRE SHIELD

1700

This upgrade generates fire shields around Spyro when he uses his Flameball attack.

EXPLODING FIREBLAST

2200

Spyro's central Flameball ignites into an explosive force that not only does more damage but also hits multiple enemies.

THE DAYBRINGER FLAME

3000

Hold down your primary power button to build up this attack, which generates a flame so big and bright it is said to bring daylight to the sky.

BLITZ SPYRO
This upgrade path lets you further develop your Charging attacks.

STUN CHARGE

1700

Enemies hit by Spyro's Charge become temporarily stunned.

COMET DASH

2200

A magic aura surrounds Spyro's horns imbuing them with extra power and damage that burns enemies in its path.

IBEX'S WRATH CHARGE

3000

Find Spyro's extra gear. With this upgrade, Spyro builds up speed and such a destructive force that it causes the very air around him to ignite into the magical form of fiery Ibex horns.

DOUBLE TROUBLE

Double Trouble comes from a tropical region of Skylands where he scoured the land in search of rare substances to create brand new spells. While he was certainly pleased with some of his early work (he was particularly fond of his hovering charm), nothing captured his fascination more than the idea of creating a clone. He spent years trying to perfect the spell, but he could never quite resolve two minor problems. One - the clones always end up half his size, and two – they have a slight tendency to....explode.

STARTING STATS

♥	MAX HEALTH	250
⚡	SPEED	35
♥	ARMOR	18
◎	CRITICAL HIT	50
◎	ELEMENTAL POWER	32

STARTING POWERS

ELDRITCH BEAM

CONJURE EXPLODING DOUBLE

PRIMARY POWER
Press and hold your primary power button to fire a beam of energy that locks onto targets.

SECONDARY POWER
Summon a mindless double that seeks enemies and explodes.

BASIC UPGRADES

ARCANE ELDRITCH BEAM

500

Eldritch Beam attack does increased damage

CONJURE UNSTABLE DOUBLE

700

Exploding Doubles do increased damage.

SUMMON MAGIC BOMB

900

Summon a Magic Bomb.

ADVANCED CONSTRUCT TECHNIQUES

1200

Have up to 3 Exploding Doubles active at any given time.

SUPER UPGRADE
WATERWALKER

4000

Can fly over water. This upgrade requires a Soul Gem from Chapter 22, Lair of Kaos.

"CHOOSE YOUR PATH" UPGRADES

CHANNELER
This upgrade path lets you further develop your Eldritch Beam and Magic Bombs.

EXTENDED ELDRITCH BEAM

1700

Eldritch Beam has longer range and does extra damage.

MAGICAL CATACLYSM

2200

Magic Bombs do increased damage.

MAGIC ARMAGEDDON

3000

Fire off repeated Magic Bombs.

CONJUROR
This upgrade path lets you further develop your skills with Exploding Doubles.

IMBUE CONSTRUCT

1700

Shoot an Exploding Double and it increases in size and damage.

ROCKET POWERED DOUBLES

2200

Exploding Doubles launch themselves at enemies and do extra damage

SPIRIT CONSTRUCT

3000

Exploding Doubles form automatically when enemies are defeated.

WELCOME TO SKYLANDS   GAME BASICS   MEET THE SKYLANDERS   THE SKYLANDS BESTIARY   STORY WALKTHROUGH   ADVENTURE PACK MAPS

SPYRO
MAGIC

Spyro is a true hero dedicated to defending Skylands from all things evil. He's fearless and brave—a strong-willed dragon, young at heart. Spyro hails from a rare line of magical purple dragons that come from a faraway land few have ever traveled. He's been on many exciting adventures, and has a remarkable knowledge of the different lands he protects... more so than any other Skylander.

STARTING STATS

♥	MAX HEALTH	280
⚡	SPEED	50
♥	ARMOR	18
⊕	CRITICAL HIT	30
◉	ELEMENTAL POWER	25

STARTING POWERS

FLAMEBALL

PRIMARY POWER
Spyro breathes balls of flame from his mouth, incinerating enemies.

CHARGE

SECONDARY POWER
Spyro runs head down knocking over enemies with his horns.

BASIC UPGRADES

LONG RANGE RAZE

500

Enhancing Spyro's lung capacity, this ability lets Spyro shoot flameballs that travel much farther than before.

SPYRO'S FLIGHT
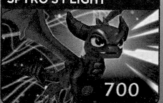
700

Spyro takes to the skies. Well, off the ground at least! Fly over water and move at great speed.

SPRINT CHARGE

900

Fitness counts. Spyro is able to charge for a longer distance with this upgrade.

TRIPLE FLAMEBALLS

1200

Shoot 3 Flameballs instead of one.

SUPER UPGRADE
SPYRO'S EARTH POUND

4000

Perform a devastating dive-bomb head smash while flying, damaging enemies all around you. This upgrade requires collection of the Soul Gem in Chapter 15, Crawling Catacombs.

"CHOOSE YOUR PATH" UPGRADES

SHEEP BURNER SPYRO
This upgrade path lets you further develop your Flameball attacks.

FIRE SHIELD

1700

This upgrade generates fire shields around Spyro when he uses his Flameball attack.

EXPLODING FIREBLAST

2200

Spyro's central Flameball ignites into an explosive force that not only does more damage but also hits multiple enemies.

THE DAYBRINGER FLAME

3000

Hold down your primary power button to build up this attack, which generates a flame so big and bright it is said to bring daylight to the sky.

BLITZ SPYRO
This upgrade path lets you further develop your Charging attacks.

STUN CHARGE

1700

Enemies hit by Spyro's Charge become temporarily stunned.

COMET DASH

2200

A magic aura surrounds Spyro's horns imbuing them with extra power and damage that burns enemies in its path.

IBEX'S WRATH CHARGE

3000

Find Spyro's extra gear. With this upgrade, Spyro builds up speed and such a destructive force that it causes the very air around him to ignite into the magical form of fiery Ibex horns.

VOODOOD

A highly decorated soldier of his people, the orcs, Voodood once commanded a well-known team of dangerous warriors. After becoming its last living member, he joined the Skylanders. Ever since he was a young orc, Voodood has collected rare and interesting bones that he uses to create weapons and devices—his favorite being the grappling hook, which grants him tremendous agility in combat. When not fighting evil, Voodood is constantly searching for new and exotic bones to expand his collection.

STARTING STATS

♥	MAX HEALTH	290
⚡	SPEED	35
🛡	ARMOR	12
⊕	CRITICAL HIT	30
◎	ELEMENTAL POWER	32

STARTING POWERS

AXE REAVER

PRIMARY POWER
Swing your fearsome axe.

ZIPLINE AXE

SECONDARY POWER
Launch the blade of your axe and rapidly reel yourself in.

BASIC UPGRADES

MAGICAL TRIPWIRE BOMB	WEIGHTED AXE	TRIPWIRE RESERVES	EXTENDED BLADE
 500	 700	 900	 1200
Summon a Magic Tripwire that collapses on your enemies.	*Axe attack does increased damage.*	*Summon up to two Magic Tripwires.*	*Zipline Axe attack has increased speed.*

SUPER UPGRADE
IMPERVIOUS TRIPWIRE

4000

Magic Tripwires deflect shots. This upgrade requires collection of the Soul Gem in Chapter 21, Arkeyan Armory.

"CHOOSE YOUR PATH" UPGRADES

ELEMENTALIST
This upgrade path lets you further develop your magical abilities.

ROADBLOCK TRIPWIRE

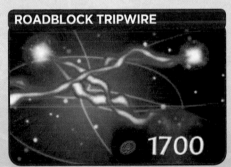

1700

Magic Tripwires are longer and do increased damage.

ELECTRIC FEEDBACK

2200

Magical energy radiates from you when hit, damaging nearby enemies.

ELECTRO AXE

3000

When you strike with your Axe, anything nearby gets hurt too.

MARAUDER
This upgrade path lets you further develop your skills with the Axe.

SHAMAN STYLE

1700

Unleash the Axe Spin combo attack.

LEGENDARY BLADE

2200

Axe attack does even more increased damage.

HYPERWIRE

3000

Zipline Axe travels much faster and does increased damage.

WRECKING BALL

Believe it or not, Wrecking Ball was once a tiny grub that was about to become the main ingredient in an old wizard's cauldron of magic soup. But when he was dropped in, the wizard was quite shocked to see the tiny grub eat all of the soup and emerge from the cauldron 20 times larger and with a long, sticky tongue. The poor old wizard was even more surprised seconds later, when Wrecking Ball proceeded to swallow him whole. Eventually he ran, quite liternally, into the powerful Portal Master Eon, who was intrigued by how he came to be and impressed with his unique abilities.

STARTING STATS

♥	MAX HEALTH	270
⚡	SPEED	43
♥	ARMOR	24
◎	CRITICAL HIT	20
◎	ELEMENTAL POWER	39

STARTING POWERS

TONGUE WHAP

PRIMARY POWER
Slap enemies with your super-tongue.

FORCEFIELD BALL

SECONDARY POWER
Summon magic for a spin forcefield charge.

BASIC UPGRADES

MAGIC BALL CONTROL

500

Forcefield Ball can be controlled and it does increased damage.

POWER BELCH

700

Release a burp attack.

TONGUE EVOLUTION

900

Your Tongue grows longer and does increased damage.

DIGESTIVE DETONATION

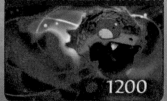

1200

Charge up your Burp attack.

SUPER UPGRADE
ENEMY SLURP

4000

Can swallow smaller enemies. This upgrade requires collection of the Soul Gem in Chapter 20, Quicksilver Vault.

"CHOOSE YOUR PATH" UPGRADES

TOTAL TONGUE
This upgrade path lets you further develop your Tongue attack.

LIGHTNING TONGUE

1700

Your Tongue can attack quicker than ever.

TONGUE GRABBER

2200

Tongue does extra damage and can pick up food and power-ups.

TONGUE SUPERMAX

3000

Your Tongue grows even longer.

ULTIMATE SPINNER
This upgrade path lets you further develop your Forcefield attack.

FORCEFIELD BLAST

1700

While in your Forcefield Ball, create a forcefield explosion.

SWATH OF TERROR

2200

The Forcefield Ball is larger and does even more increased damage.

IT'S GOTTA GO SOMEWHERE

3000

While in your Forcefield Ball, create a more powerful burp attack.

BOOMER

Originally a demolition specialist, Boomer spent his early years blowing stuff up in the Troll Enclave – something he did in his pastime anyways. But Boomer began having second thoughts about his allegiance to the Trolls when they started expanding their military because that just didn't sound as fun as blowing stuff up. So Boomer left the Troll Enclave and joined the Skylanders, determined to put a stop to the Troll Army's quest for dominance... and to blow up as many things as he can.

STARTING STATS

♥	MAX HEALTH	230
⚡	SPEED	35
▼	ARMOR	18
◎	CRITICAL HIT	50
◎	ELEMENTAL POWER	39

STARTING POWERS

DYNAMITE TOSS

PRIMARY POWER
Hurl an explosive stick of troll-grade dynamite.

TROLL SMASH

SECONDARY POWER
Smash the ground with such impact that enemies are knocked back from the furious shockwave of power.

BASIC UPGRADES

DYNAMITE FUSE FAKE-OUT

500

Dynamite does increased damage. Hold down your primary power button to delay the explosion.

BASH SMASH

700

Smash does increased damage and knocks enemies back further.

TROLL BOMB

900

Place a Troll Bomb.

TRIPLE BUNDLE DYNAMITE

1200

Dynamite does even more increased damage.

SUPER UPGRADE
TROLL BOMB BOOT

4000

Troll Bombs can be kicked at enemies. This upgrade requires collection of the Soul Gem from Chapter 5, Oilspill Island.

"CHOOSE YOUR PATH" UPGRADES

DEMOLITION TROLL
This upgrade path lets you further develop Dynamite and Time Bomb attacks.

BOMBLASTIC	TROLL BOMBS AWAY	AN ACCIDENT WAITING TO HAPPEN
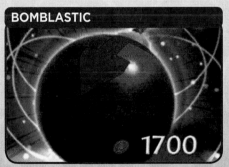		
1700	2200	3000
Troll Bombs have bigger explosions and do increased damage.	You can have six Troll Bombs active at once!	Throw 3 extra sticks of dynamite at once.

CLOBBER TROLL
This upgrade path lets you further develop your Smash attack.

HAVOC SMASH	STUPIFICATION SMASH	MEGATON CHARGED SUPER SMASH

1700	2200	3000
Smash does even more increased damage.	Smash stuns enemies.	Charge up the Smash attack, then release to do maximum damage.

DRILL SERGEANT

Like many Arkeyan artifacts, the Drill Sergeant was buried for centuries – a long forgotton remnant of a powerful civilization. It was only a chance meeting with a burrowing Terrafin that caused his systems to fire up again. By Arkeyan custom, Drill Sergeant was then obligated to become Terrafin's servant. This did not sit well with Terrafin, so his first order as master was for Drill Sergeant to not serve him at all... a command the Drill Sergeant continues to follow zealously.

STARTING STATS

♥	MAX HEALTH	290
⚡	SPEED	43
🛡	ARMOR	12
◎	CRITICAL HIT	30
◉	ELEMENTAL POWER	46

STARTING POWERS

DRILL ROCKET

PRIMARY POWER
Shoot homing rockets that chase down enemies for massive damage.

BULLDOZE CHARGE
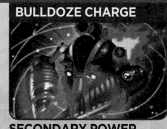

SECONDARY POWER
Charge over your enemies.

BASIC UPGRADES

A SPEEDY RECOVERY

500

Drill Rockets reload more quickly.

DOZER ENDURANCE

700

Increase the amount of time you can stay in a Bulldoze Charge.

POWER CHARGE

900

Increase the damage of your Bulldoze attack.

AUTO-BLASTER

1200

Activate your Arkeyan secret weapon.

SUPER UPGRADE
ARKEYAN ARMOR

4000

Drill Sergeant's armor becomes fortified with ancient and lost Arkeyan tech. This upgrade requires collection of the Soul Gem in Chapter 14, Battlefield.

"CHOOSE YOUR PATH" UPGRADES

BATTLEDOZER

This upgrade path lets you further develop Drill Rocket attack.

A VIEW TO A DRILL	**DX3000-DRILL DETONATOR**	**MIRV DRILL ROCKETS**

1700	2200	3000
Increase your Drill Rocket damage.	Using advanced explosive charges, this causes your drills to release an explosive area of effect pulse.	Drill Rockets explode into a series of smaller rockets.

MEGADOZER

This upgrade path lets you further develop your Charge and Auto-Blaster attacks.

SPEED DOZER BOOST	**HAIL STORM**	**MEGA DOZER**

1700	2200	3000
Bulldoze at faster speeds.	Your secret weapon just got stronger. And more secreter.	Become the ultimate bulldozer.

DROBOT

Drobot was once a small, puny dragon that was teased by other young dragons. He realized early on that he was quite possibly the smartest of his clan, and used his intelligence to assemble a robotic suit that would make him just as powerful as his fellow dragons... if not more so. His suit features laser beams that shoot from his eyes, flight enhancement technology, a vocal synthesizer that gives him a deep booming voice, and the ability to shoot spinning gears at a high velocity. With such power, he joined the Skylanders to help protect the residents of Skylands.

STARTING STATS

♥	MAX HEALTH	290
⚡	SPEED	43
🛡	ARMOR	24
⊕	CRITICAL HIT	20
◎	ELEMENTAL POWER	25

STARTING POWERS

MEGA BLASTERS

PRIMARY POWER

Shoot rapidfire laser blasts out of your eyes.

TACTICAL BLADEGEARS

SECONDARY POWER

Deploy spinning bladegears that ricochet off of walls and pummel enemies.

BASIC UPGRADES

THRUSTER FLIGHT	GALVANIZED BLADEGEARS	AXON FOCUS CRYSTALS	HOVER MODE

500	700	900	1200
Allows Drobot to fly.	*Bladegears do increased damage.*	*Eye Blasters do increased damage.*	*Allows Drobot to hover.*

SUPER UPGRADE
AFTERBURNERS

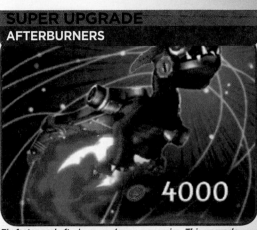

4000

Fly faster and afterburners damage enemies. This upgrade requires collection of the Soul Gem in Chapter 14, Battlefield.

"CHOOSE YOUR PATH" UPGRADES

MASTER BLASTER
This upgrade path lets you further develop your Eye Blaster attack.

DENDRITE FOCUS CRYSTALS	ANTIMATTER CHARGES	QUADRATIC BLASTERS

1700

2200

3000

Eye Blasters do even more increased damage.

Eye Blaster beams explode on contact, doing damage to enemies.

Shoot lasers out of your wings as well.

CLOCKWORK DRAGON
This upgrade path lets you further develop your Bladegear attacks.

DEPLETED URANIUM BLADEGEARS	EXPLOSIVE BLADEGEARS	TRI-SPREAD BLADEGEARS

1700

2200

3000

Bladegears do even more increased damage.

Bladegears explode on contact, doing damage to nearby enemies.

Shoot 3 Bladegears at once.

TRIGGER HAPPY

Trigger Happy is not just his name—it's also his solution to every problem. Nobody knows from where Trigger came. He just showed up one day blasting gold coins everywhere with his custom-crafted shooters. Now everyone throughout Skylands knows of this crazy "goldslinger" who will take down any bad guy... usually without bothering to aim.

STARTING STATS

♥	MAX HEALTH	200
⚡	SPEED	50
🛡	ARMOR	30
◎	CRITICAL HIT	50
◉	ELEMENTAL POWER	32

STARTING POWERS

GOLDEN PISTOLS

PRIMARY POWER
Shoot rapidfire coins out of both golden guns.

LOB GOLDEN SAFE

SECONDARY POWER
Lob explosive golden safes at your enemies.

BASIC UPGRADES

GOLDEN SUPER CHARGE

500

Charge up your Golden Gun, then release to fire a bullet that does extra damage.

POT O'GOLD
700

Throw a Pot of Gold, which does increased damage.

GOLDEN MEGA CHARGE

900

Charge up your Golden Gun longer to do even more damage.

GOLDEN MACHINE GUN

1200

Activate this machine gun and swivel its aim with the control stick.

SUPER UPGRADE
INFINITE AMMO

4000

Golden Machine Gun has unlimited ammo. This upgrade requires collection of the Soul Gem from Chapter 16, Cadaverous Crypt.

"CHOOSE YOUR PATH" UPGRADES

GOLDEN FRENZY
This upgrade path lets you further develop Trigger Happy's Golden Gun attacks.

HAPPINESS IS A GOLDEN GUN

1700

Golden Gun does increased damage.

BOUNCING BULLETS

2200

Golden Gun's bullets bounce off walls.

GOLDEN YAMATO BLAST

3000

Charge up your Golden Gun even longer to do maximum damage.

GOLDEN MONEY BAGS
This upgrade path lets you further develop Trigger Happy's throwing skills.

JUST THROWING MONEY AWAY

1700

Your Pot O' Gold attack has longer range.

COINSPLOSION

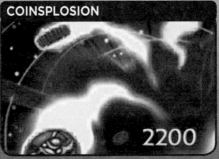

2200

Your Pot O' Gold attack explodes in a shower of damaging coins.

HEADS OR TAILS

3000

Toss a coin that does extra damage... and if it lands on heads, it does even more damage.

GILL GRUNT

Gill Grunt is one Gillman that never lets evil off the hook. For many years, the amphibian lived peacefully deep in the oceans until a nasty band of pirates kidnapped his Mermaid girlfriend. Gill then took to land and sea to search for her. He eventually joined the Skylanders to help defend the world from every kind of foe... but especially pirates.

STARTING STATS

♥	MAX HEALTH	270
⚡	SPEED	35
♥	ARMOR	6
⊕	CRITICAL HIT	50
◎	ELEMENTAL POWER	32

STARTING POWERS

HARPOON GUN

PRIMARY POWER
Shoot high-velocity harpoons at your enemies.

POWER HOSE

SECONDARY POWER
Spray water at your enemies to knock them back.

BASIC UPGRADES

THRUSTER FLIGHT

500

Allows Gill Grunt to fly.

HIGH PRESSURE POWER HOSE

700

Power Hose attack does extra damage and knocks enemies back further.

HARPOON REPEATER
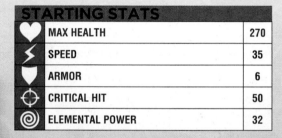
900

Harpoons reload faster.

WATER JETPACK

1200

Fly until the water jetpack runs out.

SUPER UPGRADE
ANCHOR CANNON

4000

Hold down the primary power button to charge the Anchor Cannon attack, then release to fire. This upgrade requires the Soul Gem found in Chapter 10, Treetop Terrace.

"CHOOSE YOUR PATH" UPGRADES

HARPOONER
This upgrade path lets you further develop Gill Grunt's Harpoon attack.

QUADENT HARPOONS	PIERCING HARPOONS	TRIPLESHOT HARPOON
 1700	 2200	 3000
Harpoons do even more increased damage.	Harpoons travel straight through enemies and hit new targets.	Shoot 3 Harpoons at once.

WATER WEAVER
This upgrade path lets you further develop gill your Power Hose and Jetpack skills.

RESERVE WATER TANK	BOILING WATER HOSE	NEPTUNE GUN
 1700	 2200	 3000
The Power Hose and Water Jetpack never run out of water.	Power Hose attack does even more increased damage.	When using the Power Hose, launch exploding creatures.

SLAM BAM

Slam Bam lived alone on a glacier in a remote region of Skylands, where his only friends were his many beautiful ice sculptures. It was a peaceful life, until Kaos destroyed his glacier, stranding Slam Bam on an iceberg that drifted through the skies for days. He woke up on Eon's Island, where he was taken in and trained to become a Skylander. Now his ice sculptures serve as a frosty prison for any evildoer that gets in his way, and provide a key ingredient for delicious snow cones.

STARTING STATS

♥	MAX HEALTH	310
⚡	SPEED	35
❤	ARMOR	30
⊕	CRITICAL HIT	10
◎	ELEMENTAL POWER	25

STARTING POWERS

YETI FISTS

PRIMARY POWER
Throw powerful punches with all four fists.

ICE PRISON

SECONDARY POWER
Hold the secondary power button and then release to summon an ice prison that will trap enemies.

BASIC UPGRADES

THREE'S A CHARM

500

Have up to 3 Ice Prisons activate at once.

ARCTIC EXPLOSION

700

Ice Prisons explode and damage nearby enemies.

YETI ICE SHOE SLIDE

900

Slide across the ground.

ICE KNUCKLES

1200

Punch attacks do increased damage.

SUPER UPGRADE
YETI-COOLING FACTOR

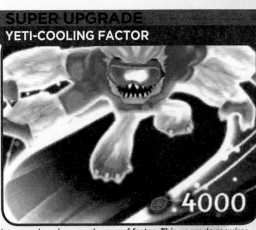

4000

Increased coolness and can surf faster. This upgrade requires collection of the Soul Gem in Empire of Ice.

"CHOOSE YOUR PATH" UPGRADES

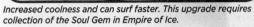

BLIZZARD BRAWLER
This upgrade path lets you further develop your Yeti Fists attacks.

BRAWLER COMBOS	**ICE MACE**	**BLIZZARD BATTLE ARMOR**
 1700	 2200	 3000
Attack with Ice Hammer.	*Punch attacks do even MORE increased damage.*	*Battle Armor makes it harder for enemies to hit you.*

GLACIER YETI
This upgrade path lets you further develop your Ice Prison attacks.

DEEP CHILL ICE COFFIN	**GLACIER TACTICS**	**WORK OF ICE ART**
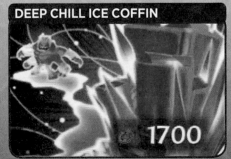 1700	 2200	 3000
Ice Prisons damage enemies trapped inside them.	*Ice Prisons travel further and faster.*	*Ice Prisons last longer and are more resistant to attacks.*

WHAM-SHELL

Wham-Shell was the long-standing king of a crustacean dominion deep in oceans of Skylands that for centuries was thought to be just legend. That is, until his underwater utopia was discovered and invaded by an oil-drilling Troll brigade that scattered his people to the wind. Armed with a magical mace that had been handed down from one king to the next for centuries, Wham-Shell joined the Skylanders to help defend the world from this type of atrocity ever happening again.

STARTING STATS

♥	MAX HEALTH	300
⚡	SPEED	50
♡	ARMOR	18
⊕	CRITICAL HIT	30
◎	ELEMENTAL POWER	39

STARTING POWERS

MALACOSTRACAN MACE	STARFISH BULLETS

PRIMARY POWER	**SECONDARY POWER**
Swing your big mace at enemies.	*Your mace shoots starfish bullets.*

BASIC UPGRADES

STARFISHICUS GIGANTICUS

500

Charge up your Starfish attack.

KING'S MACE

700

Mace attack does increased damage.

STARFISHICUS SUPERIORALIS

900

Starfish attack does increased damage.

POSEIDON STRIKE

1200

Create an electrified field that damages enemies.

SUPER UPGRADE
CARAPACE PLATING

4000

New armor makes you harder to hit. This upgrade requires collection of the Soul Gem from Chapter 5, Oilspill Island.

"CHOOSE YOUR PATH" UPGRADES

CAPTAIN CRUSTACEAN
This upgrade path lets you further develop your skills with the Mace.

CRUSTACEAN COMBOS

1700

Unleash the Mace Master attack.

MEGA TRIDENT

2200

Mace attack does more increased damage.

MACE OF THE DEEP

3000

Create a more powerful Poseidon Strike.

COMMANDER CRAB
This upgrade path lets you further develop your Starfish attack.

TRIPLICATE STARFISH

1700

Shoot 3 Starfish at once.

SEMI-ETERNAL PURSUIT

2200

Starfish attack homes in on enemies.

NIGHTMARE HUGGERS

3000

Starfish latch onto enemies doing continuous damage.

ZAP
WATER

Zap is a water dragon raised in the seas of Skylands by a family of electric eels. Although he's friendly and well liked by most sea creatures, Zap has a longstanding feud with the dolphins. Zap regularly shocks them by accident when they ride the ocean waves together, and they don't like it. In return, Zap takes offense when they suggest the shocks are no accident... although sometimes they're right! But despite these minor differences of opinion, Zap has proven to be a true protector of the seas and of Skylands.

STARTING STATS

♥	MAX HEALTH	260
⚡	SPEED	50
🛡	ARMOR	24
◎	CRITICAL HIT	30
◎	ELEMENTAL POWER	25

STARTING POWERS

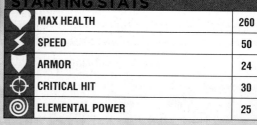

LIGHTNING BREATH
PRIMARY POWER
Spit out pure electricity.

SEA SLIME SLIDE
SECONDARY POWER
Slide on a trail of Sea Slime that enemies become stuck in.

BASIC UPGRADES

ELECTRO-SLIME
500

Shoot Sea Slimes to electrify them and shock enemies.

STAY AWHILE
700

Sea Slimes stay electrified for much longer.

MEGAVOLT

900

Lightning Breath attack does increased damage.

WAVE RIDER

1200

Summon a great wave to wash away enemies.

SUPER UPGRADE
LOVE FOR THE SEA

4000

Regenerate health in water. This upgrade requires collection of the Soul Gem from Chapter 7, Leviathan Lagoon.

"CHOOSE YOUR PATH" UPGRADES

TESLA DRAGON
This upgrade path lets you further develop your Lightning Breath and Wave attacks.

LIGHTNING STRIKES TWICE

1700

Lightning Breath bounces off of enemies, objects and walls.

ELECTRIC WAVE

2200

Wave Attack does increased damage.

TESLA STORM

3000

Lightning Breath attack does even more increased damage.

SLIME SERPENT
This upgrade path lets you further develop your Sea Slime skills.

STRENGTH IN NUMBERS

1700

Create more Sea Slimes.

CHARGED WITH PUNISHMENT

2200

Automatically electrify all Sea Slimes.

MORE ELECTRO'D SLIME

3000

Enemies take even more damage when stuck in electrified Sea Slime.

ERUPTOR

Eruptor is a force of nature, hailing from a species that lived deep in the underground until a volcano launched their entire civilization onto the crust. He's a hot head with a strong dislike for anything evil, so whenever something bad threatens his world, he quickly erupts... quite literally. To help control his temper, he likes to relax in lava pools, particularly because there are no crowds.

STARTING STATS

♥	MAX HEALTH	290
⚡	SPEED	35
♥	ARMOR	18
◎	CRITICAL HIT	30
◎	ELEMENTAL POWER	46

STARTING POWERS

LAVA LOB

PRIMARY POWER
Lob blobs of lava at your enemies.

ERUPTION

SECONDARY POWER
Erupt into a pool of lava damaging enemies all around you.

BASIC UPGRADES

BIG BLOB LAVA THROW

500

Lava Blob attack gets bigger and does increased damage.

FIERY REMAINS

700

Lava Blobs leave behind pools of flame when they hit the ground.

ERUPTION—FLYING TEPHRA

900

Lava balls shoot out while performing the Eruption attack.

MAGMA BALL

1200

Spit out Magma Balls.

SUPER UPGRADE
MEGA MAGMA BALLS

4000

Shoot up to 3 Magma Balls at a time that do extra damage. This upgrade requires the Soul Gem from Chapter 19, Lava Lakes Railway.

"CHOOSE YOUR PATH" UPGRADES

MAGMANTOR
This upgrade path lets you further develop skill with Lava Blobs and Magma Balls.

HEAVY DUTY PLASMA
1700

Lava Blobs bounce and travel farther.

LAVA BLOB BOMB
2200

Lava Blobs explode and damage nearby enemies.

BEAST OF CONFLAGRATION
3000

Lava Blobs do increased damage in the form of a fiery beast.

VOLCANOR
This upgrade path lets you further develop your Eruption attack.

QUICK ERUPTION
1700

It takes much less time to perform an Eruption attack.

PYROXYSMAL SUPER ERUPTION
2200

Eruption attack does increased damage.

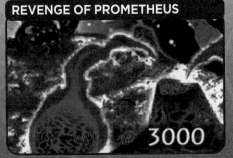

REVENGE OF PROMETHEUS
3000

Eruption causes small volcanoes to form, doing extra damage.

FLAMESLINGER
FIRE

Flameslinger is an elf archer with incredible aim. In fact, he's so good that he wears a blindfold just to prove it. When Flameslinger was young, he rescued a fire spirit from a watery doom and was gifted with two items—an enchanted bow and a pair of magical fire boots—that he now masterfully uses to defeat evil throughout Skylands. With the scorched earth Flameslinger leaves behind, you can always tell where he's been.

STARTING STATS

♥	MAX HEALTH	250
⚡	SPEED	50
🛡	ARMOR	24
◎	CRITICAL HIT	40
◎	ELEMENTAL POWER	39

STARTING POWERS

FIRE ARROW

PRIMARY POWER
Shoot flaming arrows at your enemies.

FLAME DASH

SECONDARY POWER
Dash forward, leaving a flaming path of destruction behind.

BASIC UPGRADES

SEARING ARROWS

500

Fire Arrows do increased damage.

COLUMN OF FIRE

700

Draw a circle with the Flame Dash to create a fire column. Flame Dash does extra damage.

VOLLEY SHOT

900

Fire Flaming Arrow Rain down on your enemies.

HYPER SHOT

1200

Shoot Fire Arrows much faster.

SUPER UPGRADE
SUPER VOLLEY SHOT

4000

Flaming Arrow Rain shoots more arrows that cover more area. This upgrade also requires collection of the Soul Gem from Chapter 18, Molekin Mine.

"CHOOSE YOUR PATH" UPGRADES

MARKSMAN
This upgrade path lets you further develop your Fire Arrow skills.

HELLFIRE ARROWS
1700
Fire Arrows and Flaming Arrow Rain do even more increased damage.

EXPLOSIVE ARROWS
2200
Fire Arrows explode, doing damage to anything nearby.

TRIPLE SHOT ARROWS
3000
Shoot 3 Fire Arrows at a time.

PYROMANCER
This upgrade path lets you further develop your area damage skills.

NAPALM TIPPED ARROWS
1700
Fire Arrows leave behind a burning patch, damaging enemies that touch it.

INFERNO BLAST
2200
Hold the primary power button to charge a flaming Inferno blast attack, then release to fire it.

SUPERNOVA
3000
Drawing a circle with the Flame Dash causes fire to spread out, doing more damage.

IGNITOR

On his first quest as a knight, Ignitor was tricked by a cunning witch into wearing a magical suit of armor that he was told would resist fire from a dragon. As it turned out, it was made of cursed steel. He journeyed to a dragon's lair where a single blast of fire transformed him into a blazing spirit, binding him to the suit of armor for eternity. Despite this setback, Ignitor remains a spirited knight who is always fired up to protect the lands from evil and find the witch that tricked him.

STARTING STATS

♥	MAX HEALTH	240
⚡	SPEED	43
⍰	ARMOR	12
⊕	CRITICAL HIT	40
◎	ELEMENTAL POWER	46

STARTING POWERS

FLAME BLADE

PRIMARY POWER
Swing your sword.

FLAME FORM MORTAR

SECONDARY POWER
Launch your flame spirit in an arc at foes.

BASIC UPGRADES

SCORCHING BLADE

500

Sword attack does increased damage.

FLAME FORM

700

Control your flame form after launching it.

MEGA SLAM

900

Perform a massive area slam.

FIRE AND BRIMSTONE

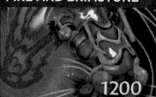

1200

Flame Form Mortar does increased damage to a larger area.

SUPER UPGRADE
FIRE FORGED ARMOR

4000

Armor makes it harder for enemies to hit you. This upgrade requires the Soul Gem from Chapter 6, Dark Water Cove.

"CHOOSE YOUR PATH" UPGRADES

SOUL OF THE FLAME
This upgrade path lets you further develop your Flame Form abilities.

DANCES WITH FIRE

1700

Flame Form moves faster and does increased damage.

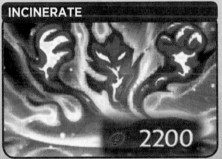

INCINERATE

2200

While in Flame Form, trigger a massive explosion.

FIRE FORM SALVO

3000

Fire two additional Flame Form Mortars that do extra damage.

BLADEMASTER
This upgrade path lets you further develop your skills with the Flame Blade.

ORDER OF THE BURNING BLADE

1700

Trigger a Fiery Burst.

DOUBLE MEGA SLAM

2200

Hold the Mega Slam attack long enough to do increased damage.

INFERNO BLADE

3000

Sword gets larger and does even more increased damage.

SUNBURN

Born in the center of an active volcano, Sunburn in part dragon, part phoenix, and 100% fire power. He is very proud of his unique heritage, and is the only dragon and phoenix hybrid known to exist in Skylands. This rare combination makes him a desirable target for greedy wizards and bounty hunters that seek to gain power by unlocking the secrets behind Sunburn's ability to teleport. Joining the Skylanders gave Sunburn a way to help defend the world from evil, but also provided him with protection, as he remains to be one of the most sought after creatures in the realm.

STARTING STATS

♥	MAX HEALTH	280
⚡	SPEED	43
♥	ARMOR	24
⊕	CRITICAL HIT	30
◎	ELEMENTAL POWER	39

STARTING POWERS

FLAMETHROWER BREATH	IMMOLATION TELEPORT
	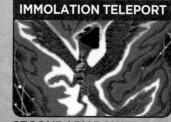
PRIMARY POWER Unleash a stream of flame breath.	**SECONDARY POWER** Teleport to another location, leaving a damaging flame behind.

BASIC UPGRADES

GUIDED TELEPORTATION	BLAZETHROWER	PHOENIX DASH	IMMOLATION INFLAMMATION
 500	 700	 900	 1200
Control the direction of your teleport.	Flamethrower Breath does increased damage.	Perform a Phoenix Dash.	Flames left behind after teleporting do increased damage.

SUPER UPGRADE
FLIGHT OF THE PHOENIX

4000

Phoenix Dash does more damage and ends with a blast. This upgrade requires collection of the Soul Gem in Dragon's Peak.

"CHOOSE YOUR PATH" UPGRADES

BLAZE DRAGON
This upgrade path lets you further develop your Flamethrower attacks.

INFINITE FLAME	**INTENSE HEAT**	**PHOENIX GRAND BLAZE**

1700	2200	3000
Endlessly use the Flamethrower Breath attack.	Hold the Flamethrower Breath attack longer for extra damage.	Hold Flamethrower Breath long enough to be surrounded by flame and do extra damage.

FLAME LORD
This upgrade path lets you further develop your Teleportation skills.

IMMOLATION DESTRUCTION	**FLAME STREAKS**	**BURNING TRAIL**

1700	2200	3000
Flames left behind after teleporting are larger and do extra damage.	Teleporting creates streaks of flames that damage enemies.	Streaks of flames do increased damage.

BASH

EARTH

Bash spent most of his early dragonhood gazing into the sky, watching the flying creatures of Skylands soar amongst the clouds. Determined to join them, he learned how to curl himself into a ball and roll with incredible momentum in a vain attempt to take flight. Over the years, his skin hardened, forming a natural protective armor unlike any other creature. Bash now thunders through Skylands, leaving a wake of destruction through any who threaten it. Despite his thick skin, Bash still gets a bit touchy about his inability to fly.

STARTING STATS

♥	MAX HEALTH	310
⚡	SPEED	35
♡	ARMOR	12
⊕	CRITICAL HIT	20
◎	ELEMENTAL POWER	32

STARTING POWERS

TAIL SWIPE

ROCK AND ROLL

PRIMARY POWER
Swing your tail around to attack a full 360 degrees of enemies.

SECONDARY POWER
Roll into a ball then bowl over your enemies.

BASIC UPGRADES

TENNIS TAIL

500

Deflect incoming objects with your Tail Swipe

IRON TAIL

700

Tail Swipe does increased damage.

SUMMONING: STONE PROJECTION

900

Summon a rock wall and then hit it with your tail to launch rocks.

DOUBLE ROLL

1200

Use the Roll attack for twice as long.

SUPER UPGRADE
TRICERATOPS HONOR GUARD

4000

New armor makes you harder to hit. This upgrade requires collection of the Soul Gem from Chapter 9, Stonetown.

"CHOOSE YOUR PATH" UPGRADES

GRANITE DRAGON
This upgrade path lets you further develop your Tail Swipe attack.

MACE OF DESTRUCTION

1700

Tail Swipe does more increased damage.

SUMMONING: STONE UPPERCUT

2200

Stone Projection does increased damage.

GAIA HAMMER

3000

Hold down the primary power button to charge up the Tail Swipe to do extra damage.

PULVER DRAGON
This upgrade path lets you further develop your Roll attack.

PULVER ROLL

1700

Roll attack does increased damage.

EARTHEN FORCE ROLL

2200

Roll does more damage and can roll right through enemy attacks.

CONTINENTAL BOULDER

3000

Roll form becomes huge while rolling. You roll faster and do even more damage.

DINO-RANG

Dino-Rang has no home and no knowledge of how he arrived in Skylands. He wanders the lands – having resolved to find the fabled Twin Diamond Boomerangs, as he believes finding them will unlock the key to his origins. Dino-Rang is unlike most unruly dinosaurs, usually maintaining a calm, collected demeanor. However, if anyone makes the mistake of calling him a dragon, Dino-Rang will lose his cool, resulting in a furious display of whirling boomerangs.

STARTING STATS

♥	MAX HEALTH	300
⚡	SPEED	43
♡	ARMOR	30
⊕	CRITICAL HIT	30
◎	ELEMENTAL POWER	39

STARTING POWERS

STONE BOOMERANGS	BOOMERANG SHIELD

PRIMARY POWER	**SECONDARY POWER**
Throw boomerangs at your enemies.	Throw both boomerangs around you in a circle for a close-ranged attack.

BASIC UPGRADES

BASALT BOOMERANGS	BOOMERANG FINESSE	STONEFIST TRAPS	DERVISH SHIELD
 500	 700	900	 1200
Boomerangs do increased damage.	Control boomerangs in the air.	Summon two Stonefist Traps from beneath the earth.	Boomerang Shield does extra damage and blocks enemies' shots.

SUPER UPGRADE
STICKY BOOMERANGS

4000

Boomerangs pick up treasure, food, and powerups. This upgrade requires collection of the Soul Gem from Chapter 6, Dark Water Cove.

"CHOOSE YOUR PATH" UPGRADES

GRAND BOOMERANG MASTER
This upgrade path lets you further develop Boomerang attacks.

VOLCANIC GLASS BOOMERANGS

1700

Boomerangs do even more increased damage.

DANCING BOOMERANGS

2200

Boomerangs bounce off of walls and enemies.

IT'S ALL IN THE WRIST

3000

Boomerang Shield lasts longer and does extra damage.

EARTHEN AVENGER
This upgrade path lets you further develop your defensive traps and abilities.

QUAD STONEFIST TRAP

1700

Summon 4 Stonefist Traps at once.

OBSIDIAN ARMOR

2200

Improved armor makes it harder for enemies to hit you.

FIST TRAP FUNERAL

3000

Enemies defeated by Boomerangs spawn Stonefist Traps.

PRISM BREAK

Prism Break was once a fearsome rock golem who didn't like to be disturbed. Then, an accidental cave-in left him buried underground. One hundred years later, a Mabu mining expedition digging for valuable jewels discovered him by chance... with a well-placed blow from a pick axe that Prism Break would rather not discuss. After 100 years of solitude, he found that the pressure of the earth had transformed him, turning his crude rocky arms into incredible gems with powerful energy. From that day forward, he dedicated himself to protecting the Mabu and Skylands alongside the other Skylanders.

STARTING STATS

♥	MAX HEALTH	290
⚡	SPEED	35
⍟	ARMOR	18
⊕	CRITICAL HIT	30
◎	ELEMENTAL POWER	25

STARTING POWERS

ENERGY BEAM

SUMMON CRYSTAL SHARD

PRIMARY POWER
Press and hold the primary power button to fire a powerful energy beam.

SECONDARY POWER
Summon crystal shards to smash enemies and refract your Energy Beam.

BASIC UPGRADES

SUPER CRYSTAL SHARD	CRYSTAL ERUPTION	EMERALD ENERGY BEAM	CHAINED REFRACTIONS

500   **700**   **900**   **1200**

Summoned Crystal Shards do increased damage.

Summon a damaging ring of crystals around you

Energy Beam attack does extra damage.

Split Energy Beams split again if they pass through a Crystal Shard.

SUPER UPGRADE
SHARD SOUL PRISON

4000

Crystal Gems form at defeated enemies. This upgrade requires collection of the Soul Gem from Chapter 8, Crystal Eye Castle.

"CHOOSE YOUR PATH" UPGRADES

CRYSTALEER

This upgrade path lets you further develop your defensive Crystal abilities.

MASSIVE CRYSTAL ERUPTION

1700

Crystal Eruption attack does increased damage and covers a larger area.

TRIPLE CRYSTAL SHARD

2200

Summon three Crystal Shards at once.

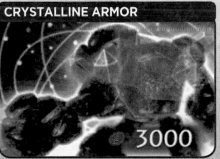

CRYSTALLINE ARMOR

3000

This armor makes it harder for enemies to hit you.

PRISMANCER

This upgrade path lets you further develop your Energy Beam attacks.

GOLDEN DIAMOND ENERGY BEAM

1700

Energy Beam attack does even more increased damage.

TRIPLE REFRACTED BEAM

2200

Energy Beam splits into 3 beams when refracted through a Crystal Gem

FOCUSED ENERGY

3000

Energy Beam attack has increased range.

TERRAFIN

EARTH

Terrafin hails from the Dirt Seas, where it is common to swim, bathe, and even snorkel beneath the ground. But a powerful explosion in the sky above the Dirt Seas turned the ocean of sand into an enormous sheet of glass, putting an end to Terrafin's duty as the local lifeguard. He then set off in search of new adventures, earning treasure by competing in local battle arenas, until his talent for brawling was discovered by Eon, a great Portal Master, who recruited him into the Skylanders.

STARTING STATS

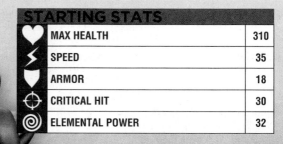

♥	MAX HEALTH	310
⚡	SPEED	35
♡	ARMOR	18
⊕	CRITICAL HIT	30
◎	ELEMENTAL POWER	32

STARTING POWERS

PUNCH	EARTH SWIM

PRIMARY POWER	**SECONDARY POWER**
Punch the enemy.	*Burrow and while underground, to perform a bellyflop.*

BASIC UPGRADES

BRASS KNUCKLES	MEGA BELLYFLOP	FEEDING FRENZY	MULTI TARGET PUNCHES
 500	 700	 900	 1200
Punch attacks do increased damage.	*Belly Flop does increased damage and affects a larger area.*	*Spawn mini-sharks that burrow and latch onto enemies.*	*Punch attack hits multiple enemies*

SUPER UPGRADE
SURFACE FEEDER

4000

Collect powerups while burrowed. This upgrade requires collection of the Soul Gem in Pirate Seas.

"CHOOSE YOUR PATH" UPGRADES

SANDHOG
This upgrade path allows you to further develop your Burrowing abilties.

MASTER EARTH SWIMMER

1700

Increased speed while burrowing.

HOMING FRENZY

2200

Mini-sharks home in on enemies and do extra damage.

RAZORFIN

3000

While burrowed, your dorsal fins do damage to enemies.

BRAWLER
This upgrade path allows you to further develop your Punch attacks.

PUGILIST

1700

Perform a Body Slam.

SPIKED KNUCKLES

2200

All punch attacks do even MORE damage.

FRENZY SHIELD

3000

You launch mini-sharks at enemies who damage you.

CAMO LIFE

Hatched at the roots of the Tree of Life, Camo is half-dragon, half-plant, with effervescent life energy flowing through his scaly leaves. This power allows him to cultivate fruits and vegetables at a highly-accelerated rate, which causes them to explode when they ripen, which makes eating them particularly challenging. Camo's unique gift caught the eye of Eon, initially because he was hungry. But upon realizing his true power, Eon convinced Camo to help the Skylanders protect their world.

STARTING STATS

♥	MAX HEALTH	300
⚡	SPEED	50
🛡	ARMOR	34
⊕	CRITICAL HIT	30
◎	ELEMENTAL POWER	39

STARTING POWERS

SUN BURST

PRIMARY POWER
Blast enemies with concentrated life energy in the form of a tiny sun.

FIRECRACKER VINES

SECONDARY POWER
Conjure a vine of rapid growth and incredibly explosive bounty.

BASIC UPGRADES

SEARING SUN BLAST

500

Sun Blast does increased damage.

MELON FOUNTAIN

700

Send Melons flying everywhere.

FIRECRACKER FOOD

900

Firecracker Vines do increased damage.

VIGOROUS VINES

1200

Firecracker Vines move quicker and further.

60

SUPER UPGRADE
ORBITING SUN SHIELD

4000

Create a Sun Blast Shield. This upgrade requires the Soul Gem from Chapter 13, Goo Factory.

"CHOOSE YOUR PATH" UPGRADES

VINE VIRTUOSO
This upgrade path lets you further develop your Firecracker Vines.

MARTIAL BOUNTY

1700

Firecracker Vines create more exploding melons.

PEPPERS OF POTENCY

2200

Firecracker Vines do even more increased damage.

PROLIFERATION

3000

Create 2 Firecracker Vines at once.

MELON MASTER
This upgrade path lets you further develop you Melon Fountain abilities.

RING OF MIGHT

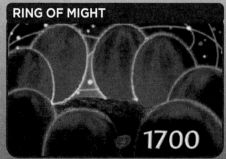

1700

The Melon Fountain blasts out more melons.

MELON GMO

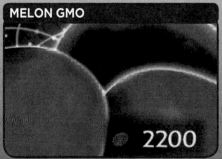

2200

The Melon Fountain does increased damage.

MELON FORTRESS

3000

Hide in the Melon Fountain, then send Melons flying.

STEALTH ELF

Stealth Elf was separated from her parents when she was very young and taken in by an unusually stealthy, ninja-like tree creature in the deep forest. Under his tutelage, Stealth Elf has spent the majority of her life training in the art of stealth fighting. After completing her training, she became a Skylander and set out into the world to uncover the mystery behind her origins.

STARTING STATS

♥	MAX HEALTH	270
⚡	SPEED	50
🛡	ARMOR	12
⊕	CRITICAL HIT	50
◎	ELEMENTAL POWER	46

STARTING POWERS

BLADE SLASH

STEALTHIER DECOY

PRIMARY POWER
Slice up your enemies with a pair of sharp blades.

SECONDARY POWER
Disappear completely but leave behind a decoy image that enemies are drawn to.

BASIC UPGRADES

STRAW POOK SCARECROW

500

A Scarecrow appears in place of your decoy and distracts enemies.

DRAGONFANG DAGGER

700

Blades do increased damage.

STURDY SCARECROW

900

Scarecrows last longer and take more damage to destroy.

ARBOREAL ACROBATICS

1200

Perform a quick acrobatic move.

SUPER UPGRADE
SYLVAN REGENERATION

4000

Regenerate health over time. This upgrade requires collection of the Soul Gem in Chapter 11, Falling Forest.

"CHOOSE YOUR PATH" UPGRADES

POOK BLADE SAINT
This upgrade path lets you further develop your blade attaks.

ELF JITSU

1700

Produce Poison Spores.

ELVEN SUNBLADE

2200

Blade attack does even more increased damage.

SHADOWSBANE BLADE DANCE

3000

Magical Blades fight alongside of you.

FOREST NINJA
This upgrade path lets you further develop your Scarecrow skills.

SCARE-CRIO TRIO

1700

Three Scarecrows are created in place of your decoy.

SCARECROW BOOBY TRAP

2200

Scarecrows explode and damage enemies.

SCARECROW SPIN SLICER

3000

Scarecrows have axes and do extra damage.

STUMP SMASH

Stump Smash was once a magical tree creature that spent most of his time sleeping peacefully in the forests of Skylands. Then one day he awoke to discover that his entire forest had been chopped down, logged clean by the Trolls... himself included! His long branches were gone, leaving him with only powerful mallets for hands—mallets he immediately put to use in smashing the Troll tree-cutting machines. Although still grumpy about what happened to him, Stump Smash has vowed to protect Skylands against those who would do it harm... especially Trolls.

STARTING STATS

❤	MAX HEALTH	340
⚡	SPEED	43
🛡	ARMOR	30
⊕	CRITICAL HIT	20
◎	ELEMENTAL POWER	46

STARTING POWERS

PULVERIZE

PRIMARY POWER
Uncork a Stumpfist smash.

WHEN ACORNS ATTACK

SECONDARY POWER
Spit acorns at your foes to slow them down.

BASIC UPGRADES

PETRIFIED PUMMEL

500

Stumpfist attacks do increased damage.

SPINY ACORNS

700

Acorns are spiny and thus do increased damage.

MEGANUT

900

Create a Meganut that damages any enemy it touches.

THORNBARK
1200

Thorns shoot out when you are hit, damaging all nearby enemies.

SUPER UPGRADE
WATERLOGGED

4000

You can float and regain health in water. This upgrade requires collection of the Soul Gem in Chapter 2, Perilous Pastures.

"CHOOSE YOUR PATH" UPGRADES

SMASH 'N BASH
This upgrade path lets you further develop Stumpfist attacks.

STUMP CRUSHER COMBOS

1700

Trigger a powerful Stumpfist Charge.

ACORN CROQUET

2200

When facing a Meganut, send it flying at your enemies.

SMASH MEGANUT

3000

When facing a Meganut, detonate it and damage enemies.

NUT CRAFTER
This upgrade path lets you further develop your Acorn and Megacorn abilities.

POLLEN PLUME

1700

Acorns explode, growing plants on all nearby enemies.

MEGANUT PROPAGATION

2200

When facing a Meganut, make it burst into acorns.

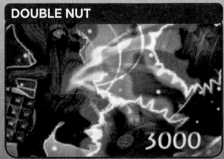

DOUBLE NUT

3000

Spit 2 Acorns at once!

ZOOK

LIFE

Zook is the wandering hero of the forests, seeking peace, tranquility and interesting things to blow up with his hand-carved bamboo tube. He uses his multi-purpose bamboo tube for pretty much everything, including a telescope and a didgeridoo... and, of course, a bazooka, which fires special explosive thorns grown in a secret bramble patch known only to his people – the Bambazookers.

STARTING STATS

♥	MAX HEALTH	260
⚡	SPEED	43
♡	ARMOR	30
⊕	CRITICAL HIT	20
◎	ELEMENTAL POWER	46

STARTING POWERS

BAZOOKA ATTACK

FOLIAGE BARRIER

PRIMARY POWER
Press your primary power button to fire Bazooka Shells that explode into shrapnel. Hold down the button to extend the range.

SECONDARY POWER
Grow a barricade made of plants to protect yourself.

BASIC UPGRADES

HARDWOOD SHELLS	FUNGAL BLOOM	MORTAR ATTACK	FULL SPLINTER JACKET

 **500**

 **700**

 **900**

 **1200**

Bazooka shells and shrapnel do increased damage.

Barrier is stronger and takes longer for enemies to destroy.

Launch a Mortar attack.

Bazooka shells create more shrapnel.

SUPER UPGRADE
MIRV MORTAR

4000

Mortar shells explode into 3 smaller shells. This upgrade requires collection of the Soul Gem from Chapter 12, Troll Warehouse.

"CHOOSE YOUR PATH" UPGRADES

ARTILLERYMAN
This upgrade path lets you further develop your Bazooka attacks.

HIGH VELOCITY SHRAPNEL
1700

Bazooka shrapnel has longer range.

OLD GROWTH BAZOOKA
2200

Bazooka shells and shrapnel do even more increased damage.

EXPLODING SHRAPNEL
3000

Bazooka shrapnel explodes on contact, damaging nearby enemies.

FLORAL DEFENDER
This upgrade path lets you further develop your Barrier and Cactus abilities.

CACTUS BARRIER
1700

Barrier does damage to any enemy that touches it.

MORTAR OF LIFE
2200

Mortar attack grows a Cactus where the shell explodes.

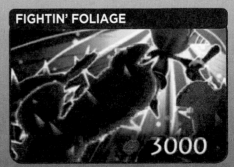

FIGHTIN' FOLIAGE
3000

Barriers and Cacti knock enemies back and do damage.

CHOP CHOP

Chop Chop is a relentless, highly skilled warrior who wields a sword and shield made of an indestructible metal. He was once an Elite Guard amongst the ancient Arkeyan beings. The Arkeyans had created massive armies of synthetic soldiers, and the Elites were the most powerful of these. Like many of the Arkeyans, Chop Chop was created from a hybrid of elements—in his case, using undead magic and technology. Refusing to believe that his people had disappeared, Chop Chop was scouring the kingdom seeking an Arkeyan leader for his next set of orders when Eon found and recruited him as a Skylander.

STARTING STATS

♥	MAX HEALTH	300
⚡	SPEED	50
▼	ARMOR	24
⊕	CRITICAL HIT	10
◎	ELEMENTAL POWER	39

STARTING POWERS

ARKEYAN BLADE

PRIMARY POWER
Slash away at your enemies with this ancient blade.

ARKEYAN SHIELD

SECONDARY POWER
Hold the button shown to protect yourself from most attacks, and deflect projectiles as well.

BASIC UPGRADES

SPIKED SHIELD BASH	VAMPIRIC AURA	SHIELD SPARTAN	BONE BRAMBLER
 500	700	900	 1200
Shield Bash an enemy.	*Sword does extra damage and Chop Chop regains health by defeating enemies.*	*Move faster and block more damage.*	*Attack enemies with damaging Bone Brambles.*

SUPER UPGRADE
CURSED BONE BRAMBLER

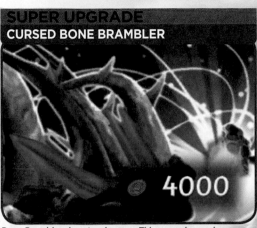

4000

Bone Brambles do extra damage. This upgrade requires collection of the Soul Gem from Chapter 1, Shattered Island.

"CHOOSE YOUR PATH" UPGRADES

VAMPIRIC WARRIOR
This upgrade path lets you further develop your Sword attacks.

ARKEYAN COMBAT MASTER

1700

Unleash the spinning Arkeyan Cyclone attack.

ARKEYAN VORPAL BLADE

2200

Sword attacks do even more increased damage.

DEMON BLADE OF THE UNDERWORLD

3000

Swords have longer range and do maximum damage.

UNDEAD DEFENDER
This upgrade path lets you further develop abilities with the Shield.

ARKEYAN SPECTRAL SHIELD

1700

Absorb and release incoming damage.

SHIELD STUN BASH

2200

Shield Bash attacks also stun enemies.

DEMON SHIELD OF THE SHADOWS

3000

Shield Bash does extra damage... and absorbed damage is automatically released.

CYNDER

UNDEAD

While just an egg, Cynder was stolen by the henchmen of an evil dragon named Malefor and trained to do his bidding. For years, she spread fear throughout the land until she was defeated and freed from the grip of the evil dragon. But dark powers still flow through her, and despite her desire to make amends for her past, most Skylanders try to keep a safe distance... because she can still be a little menacing.

STARTING STATS

♥	MAX HEALTH	260
⚡	SPEED	43
🛡	ARMOR	18
◎	CRITICAL HIT	30
◎	ELEMENTAL POWER	39

STARTING POWERS

SPECTRAL LIGHTNING

SHADOW DASH

PRIMARY POWER
Press and hold your primary power button to shock enemies with bolts of lightning.

SECONDARY POWER
Dash forward in shadow form. Ghost allies are summoned in your wake.

BASIC UPGRADES

CYNDER FLIGHT
500
Press the button shown to fly.

BLACK LIGHTNING
700
Spectral Lightning does increased damage.

DOUBLE SPOOKY!
900
Ghosts do increased damage.

SHADOW REACH
1200
Shadow Dash Range is increased.

70

SUPER UPGRADE
HAUNTED ALLY

4000

A ghost ally travels with you and damages enemies. This upgrade requires collection of the Soul Gem from Chapter 18, Molekin Mine.

"CHOOSE YOUR PATH" UPGRADES

NETHER WELDER
This upgrade path lets you further develop your Spectral Lightning attack.

UNSTABLE FORCES

1700

Hitting a ghost with Spectral Lightning makes it explode, damaging enemies.

BREATH CONTROL

2200

Spectral Lightning hold duration is increased.

BREATH OF POWER

3000

Spectral Lightning damages enemies in a larger area.

SHADOWDANCER
This upgrade path lets you further develop your abilities with Ghosts and Shadow Dash.

DEATH BOUND
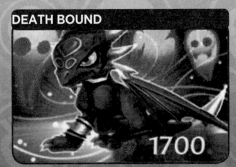

1700

Enemies hit by ghosts move slower.

GHOST HAUNTER

2200

Ghosts last longer and have a greater attack range.

SHADOW STRIKE

3000

Shadow Dash does damage to enemies.

GHOST ROASTER

Ghost Roaster is a boney ghoul with an undying appetite for lost souls. But his tendency to devour ghosts has made him a bit unpopular with the undead crowd. After eating an entire spectral village, its Ethereal Ruler, who happened to be away at the time, chained Ghost Roaster to a spiked ball as punishment. Its rattle can be heard as he wanders the night, serving as a warning to nearby spirits. In his defense, Ghost Roaster only eats bad ghosts... but even bad ghosts are deliciously good.

STARTING STATS

♥	MAX HEALTH	280
⚡	SPEED	43
▽	ARMOR	24
⊕	CRITICAL HIT	20
◎	ELEMENTAL POWER	25

STARTING POWERS

CHAIN WHIP

PRIMARY POWER
Swing your chain whip tail at enemies.

SKULL CHARGE
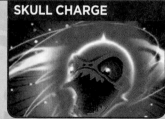

SECONDARY POWER
Transform into a ghostly skull that barrels through enemies.

BASIC UPGRADES

PAIN CHAIN

500

Chain Whip attacks do increased damage.

METALHEAD

700

The Skull Charge attacks last longer.

ECTOPLASM MODE

900

Enter Ectoplasm Mode and be immune to all attacks, but lose health over time.

HAUNT

1200

Defeating an enemy with the Chain Whip turns them into a ghost that attacks other enemies.

SUPER UPGRADE
LINGERING CURSE

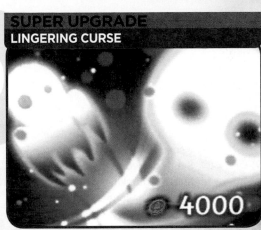

4000

Ghosts have a bigger attack range and knock enemies away. This upgrade requires collection of the Soul Gem in Darklight Crypt.

"CHOOSE YOUR PATH" UPGRADES

FEAR EATER
This upgrade path lets you further develop your Ectoplasmic abilities.

PHASE SHIFT BURST

1700

All nearby enemies take damage when you enter Ectoplasm Mode.

ECTO-FRIENDLY

2200

While in Ectopalsm Mode, you move faster and lose less health over time.

NIGHTMARE TOUCH

3000

Touching a ghost while in Ectoplasm Mode creates a powerful explosion

SKULL MASTER
This upgrade path lets you further develop your Skull Charge attack.

FRIGHT BITE

1700

Skull Charge does increased damage.

UNFINISHED BUSINESS

2200

Defeating an enemy with Skull Charge creates a ghost.

LIFE TRANSFER

3000

Devouring a ghost while doing a Skull Charge heals you.

HEX

Long ago, Hex was an Elven sorceress who traveled deep into the Underworld to confront the undead dragon king named Malefor. Though she wounded the evil creature terribly, she came back from the underworld changed – having unwillingly joined the ranks of the Undead. Many are wary of her since her transformation, suspecting that she has used her powerful magic abilities for evil purposes. But Eon trusts her, and views her as a most valuable Skylander ally.

STARTING STATS

♥	MAX HEALTH	270
⚡	SPEED	43
⌄	ARMOR	18
◎	CRITICAL HIT	30
◎	ELEMENTAL POWER	32

STARTING POWERS

CONJURE PHANTOM ORB

PRIMARY POWER
Launch magic orbs of spectral energy that track your foes.

RAIN OF SKULLS

SECONDARY POWER
Hold the button shown to begin casting this spell. When fully charged, ghostly skulls rain down.

BASIC UPGRADES

WALL OF BONES

500

Create a Wall of Bones.

STORM OF SKULLS

700

Conjure up to 4 Skulls with your Rain of Skulls attack.

BONE FORTRESS

900

The Wall of Bones is larger and takes more damage to destroy.

TWICE THE ORBAGE

1200

Shoot 2 Phantom Orbs at once.

SUPER UPGRADE
SKULL SHIELD

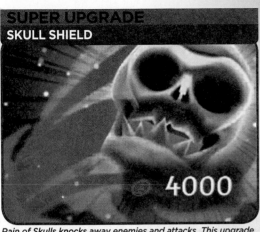

4000

Rain of Skulls knocks away enemies and attacks. This upgrade requires collection of the Soul Gem in Chapter 16, Cadaverous Crypt.

"CHOOSE YOUR PATH" UPGRADES

SHADE MASTER
This upgrade path lets you further develop your Phantom Orb attack.

LONG DISTANCE ORBS
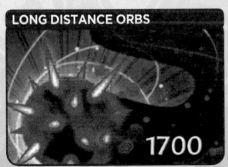
1700

Increase the range of your Phantom Orbs.

CAUSTIC PHANTOM ORBS

2200

Phantom Orbs do increased damage.

UNSTABLE PHANTOM ORBS

3000

Phantom Orbs explode, damaging nearby enemies.

BONE CRAFTER
This upgrade path lets you further develop your Rain of Skulls and Wall of Bones abilities.

COMPOUND FRACTURE
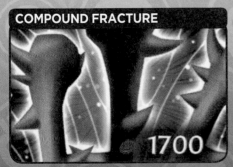
1700

Wall of Bones damages any enemy that touches it.

MASTER CASTER

2200

Takes much less time to cast Rain of Skulls and Wall of Bones.

TROLL SKULLS

3000

Rain of Skulls does increased damage.

LIGHTING ROD AIR

Lightning Rod once lived in the majestic Cloud Kingdom, where his countless acts of heroism along with his winning smile and electric physique made him the most famous storm giant in the realm. He was a true celebrity, and the palace halls were littered with adoring statues of the chisled hero. But all of the praise and admiration could never quite satisfy Rod, who yearned for something more. As luck would have it, he met an adventurous young dragon named Spyro, who told him fantastic stories of faraway places and dangers. Rod was spellbound, and he set off with Spyro to seek an audience with Eon to join the Skylanders.

STARTING STATS

♥	MAX HEALTH	290
⚡	SPEED	43
⬇	ARMOR	18
◎	CRITICAL HIT	30
◎	ELEMENTAL POWER	46

STARTING POWERS

LIGHTNING BOLT

PRIMARY POWER
Throw a lightning bolt at enemies.

GRAND LIGHTNING SUMMONING

SECONDARY POWER
Bring lightning down from the sky and control where it moves.

BASIC UPGRADES

LIGHTNING LANCER

500

Lightning Bolt does increased damage.

THUNDERATION

700

Grand Lightning attack lasts longer and does increased damage.

ZAPPER FIELD

900

Create an electrical storm that damages enemies.

LIGHTNING HARPOON

1200

Lightning Bolts stick into enemies and continue to damage them.

SUPER UPGRADE
ZAPPER FIELD DELUXE

4000

Zapper Field and clouds do extra damage. This upgrade requires collection of a Soul Gem in Chapter 9, Stonetown.

"CHOOSE YOUR PATH" UPGRADES

LIGHTNING LORD

This upgrade path lets you further develop your Grand Lightning attack.

FASTER CASTER

1700

Summon the Grand Lightning attack much faster.

ELECTRICITY CITY

2200

Grand Lightning attack has even more power and does more damage.

LIGHTNING AVATAR

3000

Summon the most powerful Grand Lightning attack ever!

TYPHOON TITAN

This upgrade path lets you create and develop defensive clouds.

CLOUD ZAPPER SATELLITE

1700

A protective cloud follows you and zaps any enemies that come near.

ZAPPIER SATS

2200

Protective zapper clouds do increased damage.

ZAPPER SATELLITE DEFENSE

3000

A third protective cloud joins you.

SONIC BOOM
AIR

Long ago Sonic Boom took refuge high atop a mountain peak in the far reaches of Skylands. Away from the mystical dangers of the outside world, she had hoped to keep her griffin hatchlings safe. But despite her precautions, a devious wizard tracked her down and placed a wicked curse on the griffin eggs. Once hatched, the young griffins can live for only mere moments before they magically return to their shells... only to be hatched again in an endless cycle. Wanting to prevent such evil from happening to others, Sonic Boom joined the Skylanders, and has trained her young to defend Skylands each time they are hatched.

STARTING STATS	
❤️ MAX HEALTH	280
⚡ SPEED	50
🛡️ ARMOR	18
⊕ CRITICAL HIT	30
🌀 ELEMENTAL POWER	39

STARTING POWERS

ROAR

PRIMARY POWER
Unleash a deafening screech!

EGG TOSS

SECONDARY POWER
Launch an egg that hatches into a feisty baby.

BASIC UPGRADES

LOUDMOUTH

500

Roar attack does increased damage.

LET THERE BE FLIGHT!
700

Your speed and armor are increased while flying.

RIDE OF THE VALKYRIES

900

Babies can now fly too. They travel at increased speed while flying.

THREE'S A CROWD

1200

Have three babies active at once.

SUPER UPGRADE
RESONANT FREQUENCY

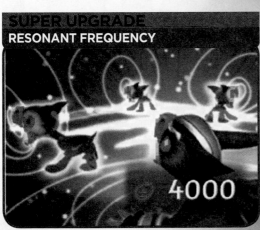

4000

Roar at babies and they will roar too. This upgrade requires collection of the Soul Gem from Chapter 3, Sky Schooner Docks.

"CHOOSE YOUR PATH" UPGRADES

MEDEA GRIFFIN
This upgrade path lets you further develop your Griffin babies.

SUNNY SIDE UP

1700

Lets you throw all three eggs at once. Eggs will knock back enemies before hatching.

SIBLING RIVALRY

2200

Have four babies active at once.

TERRIBLE TWOS

3000

Babies hatch fully grown and attack faster.

SIREN GRIFFEN
This upgrade path lets you further develop your Roar attack.

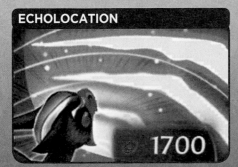

ECHOLOCATION

1700

Roar attack continues to expand on impact.

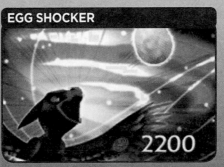

EGG SHOCKER

2200

Roar at eggs to create a big shockwave that pushes enemies back.

MORE BOOM!

3000

Increase the damage and size of the Roar attack by holding down your primary power button.

WARNADO

In the midst of a cataclysmic war between mystical forces of the ground and skies, Warnado was hatched in the fury of a powerful magical tornado, where he was trapped in an endless spin for many years. Although initially terrified and quite dizzy, with the passing years he grew to enjoy his whirling surroundings and learned various wind tricks and Elemental Air secrets. This led to him becoming a powerful force and the only known turtle of his kind. Now, the only time he gets dizzy is when he is standing still.

STARTING STATS

♥	MAX HEALTH	310
⚡	SPEED	35
♥	ARMOR	30
⊕	CRITICAL HIT	10
◎	ELEMENTAL POWER	39

STARTING POWERS

SPIN ATTACK

PRIMARY POWER
Spin in your shell to take out enemies.

SUMMON TORNADO

SECONDARY POWER
A high velocity spin generates a tornado that picks up enemies.

BASIC UPGRADES

SHARP SHELL

500

Spin attack does increased damage.

EXTEND TORNADO

700

Extend the range of your Tornado attack.

HIGH WINDS

900

Tornadoes can damage multiple enemies.

WHIRLWIND FLIGHT

1200

This upgrade provides increased speed and armor while flying.

SUPER UPGRADE
THICK SHELLED

4000

A thicker shell provides better armor. This upgrade requires collection of the Soul Gem in Chapter 4, Stormy Stronghold.

"CHOOSE YOUR PATH" UPGRADES

EYE OF THE STORM
This upgrade path lets you further develop your Spin attack and flying prowess.

LOW FRICTION SHELL

1700

Spin attack strikes farther and faster.

FLYING MINI TURTLES

2200

Mini-Warnados fly with you, and you can launch them at your enemies.

TURTLE SLAM

3000

While flying, slam down on your enemies.

WIND MASTER
This upgrade path lets you further develop you Tornado attacks.

GUIDED TWISTER

1700

Manually control the direction of your tornado attack.

SUMMON CYCLONE

2200

Tornadoes are super-sized and do increased damage.

WIND ELEMENTAL

3000

Tornadoes will attack enemies on their own.

WHIRLWIND

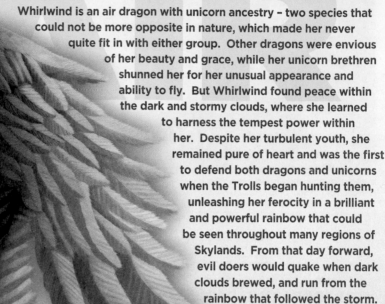

Whirlwind is an air dragon with unicorn ancestry – two species that could not be more opposite in nature, which made her never quite fit in with either group. Other dragons were envious of her beauty and grace, while her unicorn brethren shunned her for her unusual appearance and ability to fly. But Whirlwind found peace within the dark and stormy clouds, where she learned to harness the tempest power within her. Despite her turbulent youth, she remained pure of heart and was the first to defend both dragons and unicorns when the Trolls began hunting them, unleashing her ferocity in a brilliant and powerful rainbow that could be seen throughout many regions of Skylands. From that day forward, evil doers would quake when dark clouds brewed, and run from the rainbow that followed the storm.

STARTING STATS

♥	MAX HEALTH	270
⚡	SPEED	50
♥	ARMOR	18
⊕	CRITICAL HIT	50
◎	ELEMENTAL POWER	39

STARTING POWERS

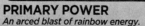

RAINBOW OF DOOM

TEMPEST CLOUD

PRIMARY POWER
An arced blast of rainbow energy.

SECONDARY POWER
Send forth clouds that electrocute nearby enemies.

BASIC UPGRADES

RAINBOW CHAIN

500

Rainbos do extra damage. Shoot a Tempest Cloud and a second rainbow chains off of it.

TRIPLE TEMPEST
700

Have 3 Tempest Clouds active. Tempest Clouds do extra damage as well.

DRAGON FLIGHT

900

Allows Whirlwind to fly.

DUEL RAINBOWS

1200

Shoot a Tempest Cloud and two rainbows will chain off of it.

SUPER UPGRADE
RAINBOW OF HEALING

4000

Rainbows heal your allies! This upgrade requires collection of the Soul Gem in Chapter 17, Creepy Citadel.

"CHOOSE YOUR PATH" UPGRADES

ULTIMATE RAINBOWER
This upgrade path lets you further develop Rainbow of Doom attack.

DOUBLE DOSE OF DOOM	ATOMIC RAINBOW	RAINBOW SINGULARITY

1700

2200

3000

Shoot two Rainbows of Doom at once.

Rainbow of Doom attack does increased damage.

Charge up a super powerful Rainbow of Doom.

TEMPEST DRAGON
This upgrade path lets you further develop your Tempest Cloud attack.

TRIPLE RAINBOW, IT'S FULL ON	TEMPEST TANTRUM	TEMPEST MATRIX

1700

2200

3000

Shoot a Tempest Cloud and 3 rainbows will chain off of it.

Bigger Tempest Cloud does increased damage with increased range.

Electricity forms between Tempest Clouds that hurt enemies.

THE SKYLANDS BESTIARY

Kaos has a large army at his beck and call and they're all found here! Use the following alphabetical listing to learn a little bit more about the enemies that try to stop you from undoing the bad deeds of Kaos.

AIR SPELL PUNK

FIRST APPEARANCE: Sky Schooner Docks

DAMAGE	59
HP	90
XP EARNED	105

ARKEYAN BLASTER

FIRST APPEARANCE: Quicksilver Vault

DAMAGE	35
HP	61
XP EARNED	61

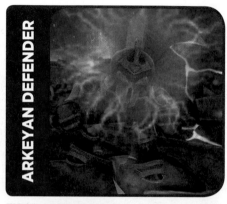

ARKEYAN DEFENDER

FIRST APPEARANCE: Quicksilver Vault

DAMAGE	71
HP	67
XP EARNED	73

ARKEYAN WAR MACHINE

FIRST APPEARANCE: Arkeyan Armory

DAMAGE	106
HP	279
XP EARNED	244

ARKEYAN ULTRON

FIRST APPEARANCE: Quicksilver Vault

DAMAGE	106
HP	279
XP EARNED	244

BLADE WITCH

FIRST APPEARANCE: Treetop Terrace

DAMAGE	33
HP	35
XP EARNED	29

BLASTANEER

FIRST APPEARANCE: Dark Water Cove

DAMAGE	24
HP	56
XP EARNED	20

BLASTER TROLL

FIRST APPEARANCE: Oilspill Island

DAMAGE	34
HP	40
XP EARNED	17

BLITZER BULLY

FIRST APPEARANCE: Treetop Terrace

DAMAGE	109
HP	149
XP EARNED	117

BONE 'N' ARROW

FIRST APPEARANCE: Cadaverous Crypt

DAMAGE	30
HP	49
XP EARNED	52

CHOMPY

FIRST APPEARANCE: Shattered Island

DAMAGE	11
HP	1
XP EARNED	1

CHOMPY POD

FIRST APPEARANCE: Perilous Pastures

DAMAGE	1
HP	61
XP EARNED	20

CONTROL TOWER

FIRST APPEARANCE: Arkeyan Armory

DAMAGE	21
HP	2
XP EARNED	4

CORN HORNET

FIRST APPEARANCE: Treetop Terrace

DAMAGE	16
HP	23
XP EARNED	29

CRUNCHER

FIRST APPEARANCE: Crystal Eye Castle

DAMAGE	16
HP	1
XP EARNED	4

CYCLOPS CHOPPER

FIRST APPEARANCE: Crystal Eye Castle

DAMAGE	48
HP	14
XP EARNED	38

CYCLOPS CHUCKER

FIRST APPEARANCE: Crystal Eye Castle

DAMAGE	36
HP	54
XP EARNED	32

CYCLOPS MAMMOTH

FIRST APPEARANCE: Crystal Eye Castle

DAMAGE	109
HP	149
XP EARNED	127

DARK AMPHIBIOUS GILLMAN

FIRST APPEARANCE: Leviathan Lagoon

DAMAGE	27
HP	298
XP EARNED	200

DARK EVIL ERUPTOR

FIRST APPEARANCE: Lava Lakes Railway

DAMAGE	98
HP	480
XP EARNED	1150

DARK ICE YETI

FIRST APPEARANCE: Leviathan Lagoon

DAMAGE	76
HP	447
XP EARNED	230

DARK IMP MINION

FIRST APPEARANCE: Creepy Citadel

DAMAGE	97
HP	361
XP EARNED	850

DARK KNIGHT MINION

FIRST APPEARANCE: Creepy Citadel

DAMAGE	80
HP	470
XP EARNED	870

DARK LIFE MINION

FIRST APPEARANCE: Falling Forest

DAMAGE	94
HP	515
XP EARNED	390

DARK MISSILE MINION

FIRST APPEARANCE: Falling Forest

DAMAGE	63
HP	294
XP EARNED	350

DARK NINJA MINION

FIRST APPEARANCE: Falling Forest

DAMAGE	69
HP	177
XP EARNED	370

DARK PHOENIX DRAGON

FIRST APPEARANCE: Lava Lakes Railway

DAMAGE	54
HP	384
XP EARNED	1130

DARK PYRO ARCHER

FIRST APPEARANCE: Lava Lakes Railway

DAMAGE	49
HP	192
XP EARNED	1100

DARK WATER DRAGON

FIRST APPEARANCE: Leviathan Lagoon

DAMAGE	18
HP	372
XP EARNED	180

DARK WITCH MINION

FIRST APPEARANCE: Creepy Citadel

DAMAGE	66
HP	397
XP EARNED	900

DEFENSE DRONE

FIRST APPEARANCE: Arkeyan Armory

DAMAGE	21
HP	2
XP EARNED	4

DROW SPEARMAN

FIRST APPEARANCE: Perilous Pastures

DAMAGE	31
HP	43
XP EARNED	38

DROW WITCH

FIRST APPEARANCE: Sky Schooner Docks

DAMAGE	19
HP	40
XP EARNED	32

DROW ZEPPELIN

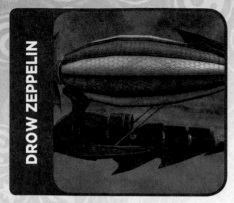

FIRST APPEARANCE: Sky Schooner Docks

DAMAGE	9
HP	10
XP EARNED	0

EARTH SPELL PUNK

FIRST APPEARANCE: Stonetown

DAMAGE	45
HP	81
XP EARNED	210

FAT BELLY SPIDER

FIRST APPEARANCE: Crawling Catacombs

DAMAGE	26
HP	67
XP EARNED	55

FIRE SPELL PUNK

FIRST APPEARANCE: Lava Lakes Railway

DAMAGE	157
HP	76
XP EARNED	335

FLAME IMP

FIRST APPEARANCE: Troll Warehouse

DAMAGE	19
HP	1
XP EARNED	4

GARGANTULA

FIRST APPEARANCE: Crawling Catacombs

DAMAGE	161
HP	186
XP EARNED	220

GNASHER

FIRST APPEARANCE: Quicksilver Vault

DAMAGE	19
HP	1
XP EARNED	4

GOLIATH DROW

FIRST APPEARANCE: Sky Schooner Docks

DAMAGE	57
HP	111
XP EARNED	128

GUN SNOUT

FIRST APPEARANCE: Troll Warehouse

DAMAGE	27
HP	187
XP EARNED	216

HOB 'N' YARO

FIRST APPEARANCE: Leviathan Lagoon

DAMAGE	73
HP	49
XP EARNED	132

LAVA KING

FIRST APPEARANCE: Troll Warehouse

DAMAGE	109
HP	105
XP EARNED	46

LIFE SPELL PUNK

FIRST APPEARANCE: Treetop Terrace

DAMAGE	87
HP	54
XP EARNED	175

MAGIC SPELL PUNK

FIRST APPEARANCE: Quicksilver Vault

DAMAGE	171
HP	81
XP EARNED	586

MARK 31 TROLL TANK

FIRST APPEARANCE: Oilspill Island

DAMAGE	53
HP	100
XP EARNED	0

MOON WIDOW

FIRST APPEARANCE: Crawling Catacombs

DAMAGE	0
HP	46
XP EARNED	66

NAUTELOID

FIRST APPEARANCE: Dark Water Cove

DAMAGE	18
HP	1
XP EARNED	4

RHU-BABIES

FIRST APPEARANCE: Cadaverous Crypt

DAMAGE	18
HP	1
XP EARNED	4

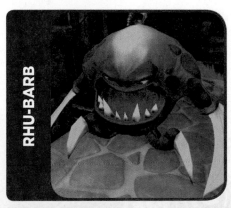

RHU-BARB

FIRST APPEARANCE: Cadaverous Crypt

DAMAGE	150
HP	200
XP EARNED	62

ROCK WALKER

FIRST APPEARANCE: Stonetown

DAMAGE	60
HP	74
XP EARNED	42

ROCKER WALKER

FIRST APPEARANCE: Molekin Mine

DAMAGE	140
HP	173
XP EARNED	152

ROCKET IMP

FIRST APPEARANCE: Troll Warehouse

DAMAGE	24
HP	63
XP EARNED	53

ROTTING ROBBIE

FIRST APPEARANCE: Cadaverous Crypt

DAMAGE	99
HP	99
XP EARNED	62

SHADOW KNIGHT

FIRST APPEARANCE: Creepy Citadel

DAMAGE	89
HP	199
XP EARNED	236

SPIDER SPITTER

FIRST APPEARANCE: Crawling Catacombs

DAMAGE	0
HP	40
XP EARNED	0

SPIDER SWARMER

FIRST APPEARANCE: Crawling Catacombs

DAMAGE	32
HP	1
XP EARNED	4

SQUIDDLER

FIRST APPEARANCE: Dark Water Cove

DAMAGE	22
HP	17
XP EARNED	21

SQUIDFACE BRUTE

FIRST APPEARANCE: Dark Water Cove

DAMAGE	91
HP	136
XP EARNED	84

STONE GOLEM

FIRST APPEARANCE: Stonetown

DAMAGE	35
HP	1000
XP EARNED	1600

TECH SPELL PUNK

FIRST APPEARANCE: Oilspill Island

DAMAGE	77
HP	90
XP EARNED	102

TIMIDCLOPS

FIRST APPEARANCE: Crystal Eye Castle

DAMAGE	36
HP	2
XP EARNED	32

TROLL GREASEMONKEY

FIRST APPEARANCE: Oilspill Island

DAMAGE	12
HP	31
XP EARNED	20

TROLL GRENADIER

FIRST APPEARANCE: Oilspill Island

DAMAGE	24
HP	18
XP EARNED	17

TROLLVERINE

FIRST APPEARANCE: Troll Warehouse

DAMAGE	89
HP	93
XP EARNED	65

UNDEAD SPELL PUNK

FIRST APPEARANCE: Cadaverous Crypt

DAMAGE	143
HP	144
XP EARNED	311

WATER SPELL PUNK

FIRST APPEARANCE: Dark Water Cove

DAMAGE	73
HP	99
XP EARNED	125

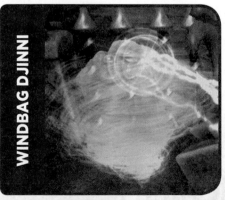

WINDBAG DJINNI

FIRST APPEARANCE: Stormy Stronghold

DAMAGE	30
HP	114
XP EARNED	70

SHATTERED ISLAND

The ancient Portal Master Eon has sent his assistant Hugo to seek your help. Place any of your Skylanders on the *Portal of Power* for transport into the game. Your hero arrives at a windmill on the outskirts (1) of a sky-island village bombarded by falling rocks. The townsfolk need help evacuating the area. Time to lend a hand!

	Treasure Chest
	Hat
	Soul Gem
	Story Scroll
	Legendary Item
——	**Direct path from Start to Goal**
——	**Optional paths for bonus items**

START

GOAL

OBJECTIVES
RESCUE THE VILLAGERS

ELEMENTAL GATES
MAGIC
WATER
TECH

AREAS TO FIND
FRACTURED VISTA
OLD TOWN
MARKET CURVE
TURTLE GULLY
TURTLE HIDEOUT
CHOMPIE PIT
WHIRLPOOL FALLS
FLOATING MILLS
ANCIENT LANDMARK

NEW ENEMIES

CHOMPY

COLLECTIONS

SOUL GEMS

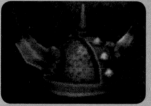

Cursed Bone Brambler
(Chop Chop)

LEGENDARY
TREASURE

Swine Salary

HATS

Viking Helmet

Pan Hat

Anvil Hat

STORY SCROLLS

Portals

While the shape and size of Portals vary, under the control of a true Portal Master, these mystic devices can connect two points in space, Dimension and, if we are to believe ancient legends, even time. Portal Masters can then send Skylanders and magic to the other side.

Portals

MISSION GUIDE

Cross the wooden bridge **(2)**. As you do, a rock smashes through the span behind you! If you walk back toward Hugo he says he'll meet you on the other side of the village where Flynn's balloon is waiting. Continue across the bridge to a new area **(3)**—the onscreen message tells you it's called "Fractured Vista."

NEW AREA FOUND

"FRACTURED VISTA"

LOOK FOR LOOT!

Use your attacks to shatter any containers or debris you find along the route. Barrels, crates, boxes, and sacks often contain jewels or other valuable items worth gold. Keep on the lookout for these items to boost your bank account. You need gold to buy upgrades!

As you proceed, another falling rock destroys a bridge to your right. Veer left instead and use your primary attack to smash through the wooden barricade **(4)**.

Continue forward until the bell-ringing Mabu, Snuckles, gives you a report. The main road out of town is blocked by debris, trapping the frightened villagers! Snuckles suggests you use the nearby old cannon to blast open an escape route.

FREE THE TOWNSFOLK

Take his advice: walk behind the cannon **(5)** and press the Action button that appears onscreen. The cannon fires and knocks down the debris. The grateful townsfolk flee to safety. Before you leave the cannon, check out the Tip on this page. Then enter Old Town.

LIBERATE OLD TOWN

In Old Town, approach the locked gate for advice from another villager, Rizzo. Move under the shining Key on the left **(6)** to grab it, walk the Key to the locked gate **(7)**, then use the controller action shown onscreen to unlock the gate. After more trapped villagers flee, step through the gate into the Market Curve area.

"OLD TOWN"

"MARKET CURVE"

LEGENDARY TREASURE!

After you blast the debris from the village gate, fire the cannon again. The second cannonball levels a small hut  on the far end of town (10), revealing a legendary treasure: Swine Salary.

Before you follow the curve to the next locked gate, turn right and nab the Treasure Chest near the fountain. Then proceed to the locked gate **(8)**, where a villager named Noobry explains that the key is near another cannon.

TREASURE CHESTS

Every chapter level in the game has three Treasure Chests loaded with gold, jewels, and other valuable items. When you find one, approach it to lift the chest in the air. Jiggle the control shown onscreen until all three of its locks break off.

When the final lock breaks, the Treasure Chest bursts open and the goodies scatter to the ground. Run around to gather everything that falls out. It's all good stuff!

Approach the cannon **(9)** and fire it to blast open another debris-clogged passage. Collect the key on the other side. See that Story

Scroll **(18)** floating on the other side of the collapsed bridge? You can't reach it now, but you can get to it shortly.

DE-TURTLE THE BRIDGES

Unlock the gate **(8)** with the key and step through to meet Nort, the villager wearing the horned helmet. After Nort explains the problem, approach the huge turtle **(11)** sitting on the bridge and push him three times to clear the way. (To push the beast, just walk into him.) More villagers liberated—good job!

NEW AREA FOUND
"TURTLE GULLY"

PUSH ARROWS

Turtle-pushing puzzles appear throughout the game. Note the blue arrows that appear over "push-able" turtles. These arrows indicate which directions you can shove the big creatures.

Continue down the ledge to the pair of turtles **(12)** lined up to block the next bridge. Push the first turtle to the left then push the second turtle completely across the bridge to the cliff wall, clearing a path. Approaching the cliff wall triggers a quick scene: Flynn hails you from above, where he waits with his balloon on a high cliff. He suggests you use the "bounce pads" to hop up to him.

Don't join Flynn yet: first, push that second turtle to the left until it drops into the ravine **(13)**, forming a bridge. This gives you access to a new area below.

ELEMENTAL GATE: MAGIC

Proceed down the slope to the rotating sphere **(14)**. This is an elemental gate—in this case, a Magic gate. Only a Magic Skylander like Spyro, Voodood, Wrecking Ball or Double Trouble can unlock it. If your current in-game Skylander isn't a Magic element hero, make the replacement now. Walk the Magic Skylander through the gate to unlock it and cross the bridge into a new area, the aptly named Turtle Hideout.

NEW AREA FOUND
"TURTLE HIDEOUT"

Approach the pack of four turtles. Push the first turtle over to the left. Push the second turtle backward twice. Now you can climb the hill on the right and acquire your first Soul Gem **(15)**. This gem makes a new power called "Cursed Bone Brambler" available for the Undead Skylander known as Chop Chop.

Next, push the turtles to clear a path to the hatbox **(16)** in the area's back left corner. To open a hatbox, you must jiggle the control shown onscreen, similar to shaking open a Treasure Chest.

EXPLORING BEYOND ELEMENTAL GATES

Only Skylanders matching the gate's element can unlock an elemental gate. However, in many cases, once the gate is unlocked any Skylander can explore the area beyond.

When the box finally bursts open, you automatically collect the Viking Helmet. When worn, this fine helm increases your hero's chance to land a Critical Hit by +5. Equip it now!

Retrace your steps back up through the Magic gate and up the slope to the blue glowing pad on the ground **(17)**.

BOUNCE PADS

Bounce pads propel you upward when you step on them. This gives you a way to ascend ledges and cliffs. Keep a sharp eye out for these blue pads as you move through the game.

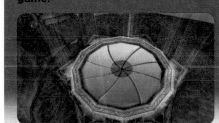

BOUNCE UP THE CLIFFS

As Flynn explained earlier, that blue pad is a "bounce pad." Step onto it to shoot upward. Don't miss the gold coins hovering in the air above! As you reach the top of your bounce motion, move forward to land on the next ledge.

Use the next pad to bounce up the next cliff, where you can collect the Story Scroll **(18)** you spotted earlier. Its title is "Portals."

STORY SCROLLS

Collect these scrolls to pick up background notes on the Skylands story plus some occasional gameplay tips.

Hop up the cliffs to Flynn **(19)** using the next two bounce pads. He points out the massive twister in the distance—it descends directly from the Darkness above!

Before Flynn can propose a plan, a huge boulder smashes into the cliff-top. Flynn escapes in his balloon but your Skylander ends up falling into the Chompie Pit below! Get ready for your first fight.

NEW AREA FOUND
"CHOMPIE PIT"

ELIMINATE THE CHOMPIES

Follow the far wall to the barred "monster gates" **(20)** where Blobbers introduces your next task: defeat the nasty Chompies that suddenly ambush your hero. You can't leave the pit until all 15 Chompies are defeated.

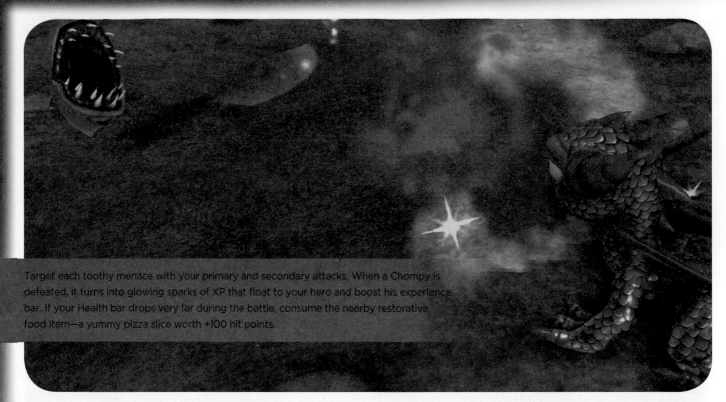

Target each toothy menace with your primary and secondary attacks. When a Chompy is defeated, it turns into glowing sparks of XP that float to your hero and boost his experience bar. If your Health bar drops very far during the battle, consume the nearby restorative food item—a yummy pizza slice worth +100 hit points.

HEALTH FOOD

Spinning food items like this pizza slice restore hit points to your hero's Health gauge. Try to consume these only if your Health rating is lowered. Otherwise their restorative effect is wasted.

When the final Chompy falls, the monster gates open. Before you leave the pit, however, cross the narrow lagoon to collect the Treasure Chest. Note that to get across water you need a Water-based Skylander like Gill Grunt. (Flying Skylanders like Spyro can glide cross water too, but if this is your first time playing Chapter 1, Spyro probably hasn't acquired his flying ability yet.)

ELEMENTAL GATE: WATER

Proceed through the gap to a pair of elemental gates. Approach the Water Gate first—the rotating sphere on the left **(21)**. Only Water Skylanders can unlock this gate. If your current Skylander isn't a Water element hero like Gill Grunt, Slam Bam, Zap, or Wham-Shell, make the change now.

DON'T OVEREAT!

Eating food restores health, but only up to your Max Health number. So if your hero has a full health gauge, leave food behind! Come back later to eat when your health is low.

Walk through the gate to unlock it then step into the whirlpool to transport to the next plateau **(22)**, a new area called Whirlpool Falls. Use the bounce pads to hop up to the top-most plateau; smash the carts, barrels, and sacks along the way to collect loot.

NEW AREA FOUND
"WHIRLPOOL FALLS"

At the top, shake open the hatbox **(23)** to get the Pan Hat. When donned, this fine piece of equipment bestows +2 Armor and +2 Elemental Power to the lucky wearer. Equip it now! Then work your way back down to the elemental gate and exit Whirlpool Falls.

ELEMENTAL GATE: TECH

Now approach the Tech Gate—the rotating sphere on the right **(24)**. Only Tech Skylanders can unlock this gate. If your current Skylander isn't a Tech element hero like Trigger Happy, Boomer, Drobot, or Drill Sergeant, make the switch now.

Walk through the gate to unlock it then cross the bridge to a new area called Floating Mills. Time your run across the next two circular platforms **(25)** to avoid the giant spinning blades. They turn slowly, but don't be careless: if they cut you, it hurts quite a bit.

NEW AREA FOUND
"FLOATING MILLS"

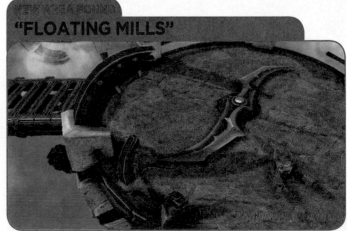

When you reach the windmill, shake open the hatbox **(26)** to acquire the Anvil Hat. Equip it immediately to gain a whopping +5 Armor boost. Then work your way carefully through the spinning blades again and exit Floating Mills.

SAVE THE MABU ROYAL FAMILY

Proceed up the ramps **(27)** to meet Blobbers again. He reports that the royal palace is gone and asks your Skylander to save the royal family. Continue up the ramp to the Ancient Landmark area **(28)** and wipe out the pack of Chompies. Push the turtle into the gap on the left so you can climb that ramp up to the next cannon **(29)**.

NEW AREA FOUND
"ANCIENT LANDMARK"

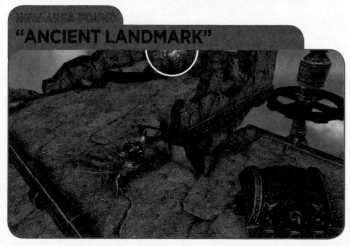

Fire the cannon to knock down the wall **(30)** across the walkway then use the bounce pad to jump across to the platform. Raid the Treasure Chest on the platform then grab the floating key. Use the key to unlock the gate **(31)**. This releases the royal family and completes the mission.

Hugo tells the story of how Skylands came to its present state. You learn about Eon and Kaos, the Core of Light, and the Skylanders' great battle against the forces of Darkness. Now you understand why Spyro and his friends need a new portal master!

2 PERILOUS PASTURES

Back at the Ruins, talk to Flynn to and select "Yes" to take the balloon to Perilous Pastures. Flynn delivers your Skylander to that destination and suggests you look for Cali. He plans to reconnoiter from the air, and takes off.

Legend

- Treasure Chest
- Hat
- Soul Gem
- Story Scroll
- Legendary Item
- —— Direct path from Start to Goal
- —— Optional paths for bonus items

OBJECTIVES
FIND CALI
RESCUE CALI

ELEMENTAL GATES
TECH
WATER

AREAS TO FIND
SUNFLOWER RIDGE
BLEATING HIGHLANDS
FAIRY RING
ANCIENT STONES
LANDING DECK

NEW ENEMIES

CHOMPY POD   DROW SPEARMAN

COLLECTIONS

SOUL GEMS

*Waterlogged
(Stump Smash)*

LEGENDARY TREASURE

Enigma Pig

HATS

Cowboy Hat

Birthday Hat

STORY SCROLLS

The problem with Sheep

A note from Hugo says, "Sheep are among the most feared creatures in Skylands. Those Mabu having fallen asleep while counting large herds of sheep, often discover their belongings missing when they wake up. When questioned of course, the sheep never admit to have taken anything."

The problem with Sheep

MISSION GUIDE

From the Start, approach the bridge to hear Eon explain how different areas of Skylands have different elemental energies. Cross the bridge to enter Sunflower Ridge, an area strong in the Tech element. (Note that the Tech icon appears onscreen in the corner.) Switch to a Tech Skylander such as Trigger Happy.

NEW AREA FOUND
"SUNFLOWER RIDGE" (TECH)

MATCHING ELEMENTS

Eon lets you know whenever you enter a zone where a particular element is strong. The elemental icon also appears in the upper left corner of your screen. When you switch to a Skylander of the same element, your character has extra power and reaps extra treasure while in that zone.

Grab the key floating up ahead **(1)** and use it to open the nearby gate. Before you go through that gate, explore the elemental area to the right first.

ELEMENTAL GATE: TECH

Use a Tech Skylander to unlock the elemental gate **(2)**. Cross the bridge into the Bleating Highlands, where you learn that the Tech element is strong in this zone—consider switching to a Tech Skylander.

NEW AREA FOUND
"BLEATING HIGHLANDS" (TECH)

Scoop up treasure and use the bounce pads to hop up platforms until you reach a plateau **(3)** with three Drow Spearmen wielding nasty-looking war scythes near some Chompy Pods. This is a tough fight for an inexperienced Skylander, so keep moving and look for health-boosting food drops.

HAY THERE!

Unleash your attacks on all the hay bales, hay carts, wheelbarrows, stick bundles, and scarecrows you find in the Perilous Pastures. They hold a good deal of loot.

Target the Chompy Pods first! You want to stop their Chompy-spawning activity to keep the fight more manageable. When you face a Drow Spearman, watch out for his big scythe windup—it gives you time to dart to the side and avoid the hit.

After you eliminate all foes, look for the coins and gems stacked in the plateau's corners then hop down to the next area **(4)** that has two blue bounce pads. Walk down to the drop-off and step off so you fall through the line of gold coins below. (The drop-off spot is circled in the image here.)

You fall to a platform **(5)** where a Chompy Pod spits out Chompies. Wipe them out, clean out the area for drop items, then use bounce pads to hop up a series of platforms to the Treasure Chest **(6)**. Shake open the chest then bounce up one more bounce pad to return to **(4)** where you first dropped off.

Now use the leftmost bounce pad to hop up to the next plateau. Slash through the stick bundles and shake open the hatbox **(7)** to acquire the Cowboy Hat. Equip it for the stat boost and continue on.

Drop carefully down the next ledge through the line of floating coins. You fall almost directly onto a Soul Gem! (This one gives Stump Smash the ability to acquire the "Waterlogged" power.) Finally, hop off the last ledge to leave the Bleating Highlands. You're back to Sunflower Ridge and the gate you unlocked with the key.

FIGHT THROUGH FAIRY RING

Push both turtles backward into the gap **(9)** to form a bridge then cross over it and grab the key just down the road.

Defeat the Drow Spearman at the gate **(10)** and use the key to unlock it. Proceed into the circular area called Fairy Ring, where the Magic element is strong. Switch your hero to Spyro or another Magic Skylander.

"FAIRY RING" (MAGIC)

Defeat the Chompy Pod and its Chompies in the ring then grab the nearby Story Scroll entitled "The Problem with Sheep." Now comes a turtle-pushing puzzle. First, push the turtle twice to clear the wall gap. Go through and fight off the pair of Drow Spearmen. Collect any items

in the area, then push the turtle back into the wall gap. Now you can cross over the turtle's back to grab the key up on the stone walkway (11).

Hop down and use the key to open the next gate. Follow the grassy path uphill to the left side of the house where the path curves (12). Switch to a Life Skylander like Stealth Elf and walk toward the cliff—magically, a Life bridge forms! Walk across to find the legendary treasure, Enigma Pig, on a small island.

Press the button near the legendary treasure to unlock a nearby door that leads to the Landing Deck area.

If you don't open the path to the legendary treasure, follow the grassy path around through two wooden fences—blast your way through both—until you reach a Treasure Chest. Shake it open to gather goodies then push the nearby turtle through the wall gap so it drops (13). Hop down and head for the Water Gate to the left.

ELEMENTAL GATE: WATER

Use a Water Skylander to open the gate and hop in the whirlpool (14) to transport up to a new zone, Ancient Stones (15). Cross the field to the stone blocks for which the area is named.

"ANCIENT STONES" (WATER)

Approach the first group of blocks and push them in the following order:

- **Push the first block at (a) over the teleport pad (b).**
- **Push the block at (c) left to (d).**
- **Push the block at (e) to (c).**
- **Push the block at (f) to (g).**
- **Push the block at (h) to (f).**
- **Push the block over the teleport pad (b) to (e).**

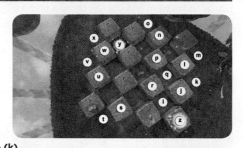

Well done! Step onto the teleport pad. This zaps you to **(i)** in the middle of the next, larger group of blocks. Your Skylander automatically pushes the block at **(j)** over to **(k)**.

- **Push the block at (l) to (m).**
- **Push the block at (n) to (o).**
- **Push the block at (p) to (q).**
- **Push the block at (r) to (i).**
- **Push the block at (s) to (t).**
- **Push the block at (u) to (v).**
- **Push the block at (w) to (x).**

Now you can step onto the teleport pad at **(y)**. This zaps you onto the plateau (at **(17)** on the map) where you can score the Treasure Chest. Here it gets tricky again! Check the image closely: you want to step gingerly off the plateau so you land atop the blocks, then very carefully follow the route shown to reach the teleport atop the block at **(z)**.

If you fall off the blocks en route, you must return to the teleport at **(y)**, zap back up to the plateau, drop back onto the blocks, and try to follow the route shown to **(z)** again.

Stepping onto the teleport atop the block at **(z)** zaps you over to another plateau (at **(18)** on the map) where you can shake open the hatbox there and acquire the awesome Birthday Hat.

Wear it if you want, then step on the nearby teleport pad to zap over to the right-side plateau (where you found the chest). Then hop down and retrace your route via the whirlpool out of the Ancient Stones area and return through the Water Gate back to the turtle at **(13)**.

FIND AND SAVE CALI

Push the turtle along the path that runs around the corner until the beast falls into the gap **(19)** then cross over its back. Follow the grassy path up the rock ramp **(20)**.

Switch to a Life Skylander like Stealth Elf if you have any. Now proceed forward into the final area, Landing Deck, a zone strong in the Life element. Your arrival triggers the appearance of Flynn in his balloon. He announces that a bunch of evil Drow have captured Cali!

NEW AREA FOUND
"LANDING DECK" (LIFE)

Clear the space around the massive cannon **(21)**—a Drow Spearmen and a few sinister Chompy Pods infest the area. After you eliminate the foes, approach the cannon and press the control shown onscreen to man the weapon (if you missed any enemies, before entering the cannon, it automatically eliminates any stragglers). Use the targeting reticle to aim at each of the four locks on the gate.

Blast off all four locks to exit the cannon, then approach the now-liberated Cali to complete the mission. But you still have a quick task to complete back at the Ruins before you can start the next chapter. Flynn arrives and flies you back to Hugo.

CLEAR ACCESS TO THE FAR VIEWER

Hugo has an announcement: he's found the blueprints for the Core of Light, the ancient device used to repel the forces of Darkness. Hugo wants to use the Far Viewer to locate the Eternal Sources needed to rebuild the core. But access to the great telescope is blocked by a

tangle of brambles. When the scene ends, simply hack or blast your way through the brambles to the Far Viewer.

When the way is clear, Hugo uses the device to spot the Eternal Air Source in the evil Drow's Stormy Stronghold. But Flynn's balloon will

need a propeller to reach the blustery destination. Cali reports that the Drow patrol the Sky Schooner Docks with their Elite Airship, a vessel sure to have a good propeller.

3
SKY SCHOONER DOCKS

Find Flynn near the balloon dock and agree to fly with him to the Sky Schooner Docks. When you arrive at the imposing airship facility, Flynn sets down on a small floating sky-island near the docks. Your task: Find the Golden Propeller.

START

GOAL

Treasure Chest

Hat

Soul Gem

Story Scroll

Legendary Item

— Direct path from Start to Goal

— Optional paths for bonus items

OBJECTIVES
FIND THE GOLDEN PROPELLER

ELEMENTAL GATES
UNDEAD
EARTH

AREAS TO FIND
GLIDER TOWER
PROPELLER FARM
FORTRESS TOWER
KAW'S ISLANDS
SHORELINE TOWER

NEW ENEMIES

DROW ZEPPELIN

DROW WITCH

AIR SPELL PUNK

GOLIATH DROW

COLLECTIONS

SOUL GEMS

*Resonant Frequency
(Sonic Boom)*

LEGENDARY TREASURE

Wild Runners

HATS

Propeller Cap

Jesster Hat

STORY SCROLLS

Fairy upgrades

For as long as anyone can remember, Skylanders have been friends with fairies. Perhaps this is because fairies can turn treasure into a kind of upgrade magic that gives Skylanders exciting new powers and abilities, plus delightfully fresh breath.

Fairy Upgrades

MISSION GUIDE

Use the teleport pad to zap across to the first skydock platform and defeat the lone Drow Spearman. Cross the bridge to the Glider Tower area—the Tech element is strong here, so switch to a Tech Skylander like Trigger Happy.

NEW AREA-SONG
"GLIDER TOWER" (TECH)

Turn right at the raised platform and follow the ramp up to the key **(1)** guarded by a Chompy Pod and a Drow Spearman. Eliminate the Chompy threat then use the key on the nearby gate. Move across the next bridge to the cannon emplacement **(2)**.

SHOOT DOWN THE ZEPPELINS

Man the big gun and start shooting down the Drow warships. Use the left stick to aim the targeting reticle and shoot by pressing the Attack button. The Drow zeppelins (the striped airships) shoot back, so keep an eye on the cannon's health bar in the center: it drops as you take hits. If it drops to zero, your Skylander gets kicked out of the cannon and you must start over.

Win this mini-game by knocking 15 Drow zeppelins from the sky—an onscreen counter keeps track of how many you nail. Another counter marks how many of the red gems you've destroyed. When you knock down the 15th zeppelin, watch as it crash-lands through the nearby gate, clearing your way forward.

WINGED GEMS

Blast as many of the winged red gems as you can with cannon fire. Each gem you nail is worth extra gold!

DEFEAT THE WITCHES

Proceed through the gate to meet your first Drow Witch **(3)**. Watch out for her deadly tosses as she flings energy-charged disks at your Skylander. These frisbee-like projectiles can be dodged, but the Witch throws one after another quickly, so always be ready for the next toss! After you beat the first Drow Witch, continue along the wooden walkway toward the elemental gate to the right. En route you face two more Drow Witches—these attack from off-screen to the right as you approach, so be ready.

ELEMENTAL GATE: UNDEAD

Unlocking this gate **(4)** requires an Undead Skylander like Chop Chop, Hex, or Cynder so change your Skylander if necessary. Unlock the gate and move across the awesome bone bridge that forms, leading to the rotating propeller platforms. This new zone is strong in the Undead element.

NEW AREA FOUND

"PROPELLER FARM" (UNDEAD)

The platforms are tricky. Propellers are razor sharp, move fairly fast, and overlap frequently. In some places you must use bounce pads to hop up levels. The best route is to keep working leftward toward the small platform that holds a key **(5)**. Carry that key back to the teleport pad at **(6)** where you can zap quickly up to the locked gate **(7)**.

Raid the nearby Treasure Chest before unlocking the gate. Bounce up to the next platform, hop carefully through the spinning propellers, and reach the hatbox. Shake it open to acquire the Propeller Cap! Now you can use the nearby teleport pad to zap back near the bone bridge and exit the Propeller Farm via the elemental gate **(4)**.

GUN DOWN THE DROW AIRSHIP

Back in the Glider Tower area, switch to a Tech Skylander. Walk to the end of the wooden walkway and blast the Chompy Pod, Chompies, and Drow Witch guarding the area. (You can use Trigger Happy's "Lob Golden Safe" secondary attack to nail all foes without hopping down off the walkway!) Then proceed to the anti-airship cannon **(8)** and hop in.

Use the weapon to gun down Drow zeppelins, then target the big Drow warship that appears. The blue-and-green striped cruiser can take numerous hits before you disable it so keep firing! When the ship finally goes down it smashes open the next gate for you.

FIGHT THROUGH THE FORTRESS TOWER

Proceed through the gate into a new zone, the Fortress Tower. Here the Air element is best, so consider switching to Sonic Boom, Whirlwind, or some other Air Skylander if you have any.

NEW AREA FOUND
"FORTRESS TOWER" (AIR)

Up ahead you face an annoying new foe, the Air Spell Punk **(9)**. This fellow doesn't have much in the way of attack powers, but he can cast protective spells on his allies! His Air Spell makes your foes immune to projectiles, so eliminate the Punk first, then turn your attention to the Drow Spearmen escorting him.

When you eliminate all three foes, the nearby gate lowers. Nab the Story Scroll (entitled "Fairy Upgrades") from the circular alcove. Then veer to the right to find the Treasure Chest behind the corner tower. Watch out for those nasty exploding plants growing near the chest, however.

Proceed down the ramp to the left where you meet a formidable combat challenge **(10)**: some Drow Witches and Spearmen protected by a spell-casting Air Spell Punk (circled in the screenshot). Try to dash through the troops to nail the Punk first if you can—he's hiding on the dirt path behind them, protected by a row of destructible items. Then clear the rest of the area to lower the next gate.

After the fight, go collect the Soul Gem in the nearby circular alcove: it unlocks the "Resonant Frequency" power for Sonic Boom. Then follow the dirt path to the Earth elemental gate **(11)**.

ELEMENTAL GATE: EARTH

Switch to an Earth Skylander such as Prism Break, Bash or Dinorang to unlock this gate **(11)**. Cross the rock bridge into the new zone, Kaw's Islands. Use the bounce pad to hop up a level then terminate the Chompy-spewing Chompy Pod and its minions. Use more pads to bounce up from plateau to plateau, collecting treasure.

"KAW'S ISLANDS" (EARTH)

Bounce up to the topmost sky-island to find a hatbox containing the amusing Jesters Hat. But instead of using the teleport pad there, step off the island's edge in the exact spot circled in the screenshot.

This lets you drop right onto another tiny sky-island below where you find a lovely Treasure Chest. Step on the teleport pad there to zap back to the connected plateaus **(12)** then exit Kaw's Islands.

MEET PERSEPHONE

Move down the ramp to trigger your first meeting with Persephone the Fairy **(13)**. Persephone will be your go-to gal for Skylander upgrades back at the Ruins, but for now, just watch as she introduces herself "extremely" and then the Drow warship docks.

DEFEAT THE GOLIATHS

Now comes a tough fight. Four Drow Spearmen rush across the warship. Take them down! When they fall, a huge Goliath Drow is released. A gate blocks the stairs behind him until you can defeat the big monster. Watch out! Whenever the Goliath crouches and glows green, he's about to charge! During this charge the big goon is indestructible and delivers much damage when he strikes. Sidestep the charge, get in an attack or two, and then sidestep the next charge. Continue this pattern until the monster falls.

Now climb the stairs and eliminate a second Drow Goliath posted there along with a pair of Drow Witches. When these foes fall, the two raised gangways drop at **(14)** and **(16)** on the far side of the ship. Now you can exit the far side of the warship to a new area, Shoreline Tower.

"SHORELINE TOWER" (EARTH)

FIND THE LEGENDARY ITEM

Backtrack across the deck and debark at **(14)** first to reach the guard tower. The tower doors open as you approach and reveal a teleport pad. Use the pad to zap over to a small sky-island **(15)** guarded by a Chompy Pod spewing Chompies. Destroy the hostile plant and use the next teleport pad to reach the legendary treasure, the Wild Runners. Hop down and return to the warship.

SHOOT DOWN THE ELITE AIRSHIP

Cross the warship's deck and exit the other lowered gangway **(16)**. Proceed to the next cannon **(17)** and use it to target the Elite Airship. Direct some fire at the swarm of zeppelins that attacks too! When you finally destroy the heavy warship it crash-lands into the last gate, smashing it open and dropping its Golden Propeller.

Cross the bridge and acquire the Golden Propeller to complete the mission. Flynn arrives in his balloon and hauls your Skylander and the propeller back to the Ruins of the Core of Light.

UPGRADE YOUR SKYLANDERS!

Back at the Ruins Flynn tells you to visit Persephone and buy upgrades for any Skylanders who've amassed gold during the missions so far. Purchase "Spyro's Flight" for Spyro if you can afford it. This power lets Spyro move much faster, and allows him to glide over water too.

FOREVER POWERS

Once a Skylander levels up or acquires new powers via Persephone, the creature retains these advances within the "brain" in its toy form. This lets you import your Skylander into games with your friends using any *Portal of Power!*

4

STORMY STRONGHOLD

Talk to Flynn and agree to fly in his propeller-enhanced balloon to your next destination, the Stormy Stronghold. You arrive to the terrifying sight of another massive tornado tearing apart the citadel! Flynn guesses that the Drow found the Eternal Air Source and are trying to harness its power. Doesn't look good, does it?

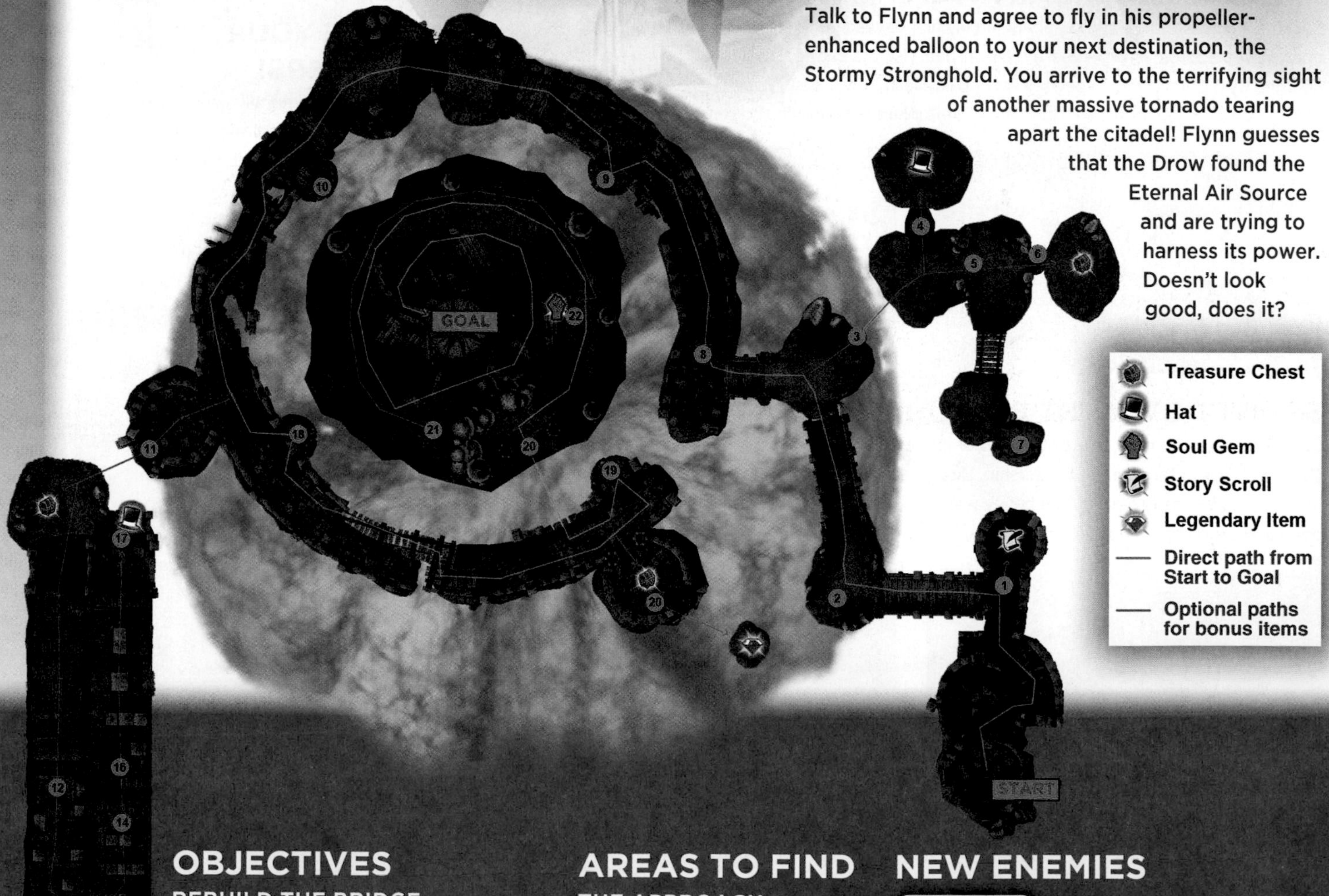

GOAL

START

🗃	**Treasure Chest**
▭	**Hat**
🔹	**Soul Gem**
📜	**Story Scroll**
✦	**Legendary Item**
—	**Direct path from Start to Goal**
—	**Optional paths for bonus items**

OBJECTIVES
REBUILD THE BRIDGE
FIND THE ETERNAL AIR SOURCE

ELEMENTAL GATE
LIFE
AIR

AREAS TO FIND
THE APPROACH
LOWER REACH
THE BATTLEMENT
SKY RAMPARTS
INNER KEEP

NEW ENEMIES

WINDBAG
DJINNI

COLLECTIONS

SOUL GEMS

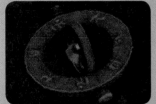

*Thick Shelled
(Warnado)*

LEGENDARY TREASURE

Ancient Carillon

HATS

Fez

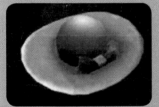

Fancy Hat

STORY SCROLLS

Tornado Sightings

A note from Hugo says, "While everybody fears large, destructive tornadoes, smaller friendlier ones are quite popular in Skylands. Mabu come from all over to throw unwanted items into the small tornadoes - things like garbage, tax forms and when possible, sheep."

Tornado Sightings

MISSION GUIDE

Flynn drops off your Skylander on a rampart and suggests you rebuild the bridge shattered by the twister. Descend the stone staircase into the first zone, the Lower Reach. See the Story Scroll glowing behind the stone wall **(1)**? Bash through the wall and grab the scroll entitled "Tornado Sightings."

NEW AREA FOUND

"THE APPROACH" (LIFE)

Cross the wooden bridge and wipe out the Chompy Pod and Chompies then use the nearby key **(2)** to unlock the gate. Maneuver around the Bounce Pods on the bridge to the next clearing where an Air Spell Punk protects the Drow Spearmen who attack your Skylander. Once you clear the area, switch to a Life Skylander and approach the elemental gate to the right **(3)**.

ELEMENTAL GATE: LIFE

Open the Life gate with your Life Skylander and cross the living bridge to the new zone strong in the Life element, called The Approach. Proceed to the three blocks.

NEW AREA FOUND

"LOWER REACH"

Push the first block into the ravine **(4)**. The ravine is three blocks wide, so push the second block over on top of the first, then push it forward until it falls into the second gap. Then push the third block off the cliff to reveal a yellow teleport pad. Step on the pad to teleport up to the second level **(5)**.

You arrive in the middle of four blocks. First, push the top block off the teleport pad. Before you use the pad, however, face left and push the leftmost block off the cliff—it drops to the plateau below (see the screenshot). Hop down to that plateau and push this newly fallen block into the remaining gap in the ravine. Now you can walk over the blocks and shake open the hatbox to acquire the Fez.

Teleport back up to the second level (5) again. Push the rightmost block into the ravine (6) and cross over to nab the Treasure Chest. Return and smash through the wooden fence to defeat three Drow Spearmen guarding a pile of treasure (7). Snag the loot and exit The Approach back into the Lower Reach.

LOWER THE LIGHTNING PYLONS

Smash through the wall into the next zone (8), The Battlement, where Magic Skylanders gain strength. Now you must work your way down a long, curving battlement walkway filled with guards and barriers. Time your run through three sets of impaling spears that shoot up from the ground at regular intervals.

NEW AREA FOUND
"THE BATTLEMENT" (MAGIC)

Continue to the glowing lightning pylon (9). Approach the pylon and rotate the control stick in the direction shown onscreen to lower the pylon, which repairs part of the stronghold bridge and also lowers the gate just ahead. Smash through the next wooden fence and get ready for a fight.

The next area is quite dangerous, featuring a Drow Witch and a Chompy Pod spitting out Chompies, plus a trio of Drow Spearmen guarding the next gate. Clear the area, smash through the fence, and then rotate another lightning pylon (10) to lower the next gate and repair more of the stronghold bridge.

Continue along the walkway, fighting past mixed Drow guards and timing your movement through another set of impaling spears. Before you reach the next pylon, however, turn into the alcove that leads to the Air elemental gate (11).

ELEMENTAL GATE: AIR

Switch to an Air Skylander like Sonic Boom to unlock the Air gate (11). Step through the gate into the whirlwind to transport across the gap to a new zone, Sky Ramparts, strong in the Air element. (If you don't step out of the whirlwind on the other side the moment you arrive, it sucks you in and transports you right back to where you started.)

NEW AREA FOUND
"SKY RAMPARTS" (AIR)

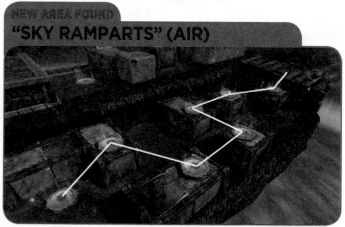

Shake open the nearby Treasure Chest and gather the goods, then move down the long corridor of impaling spike traps. Some require bounce pads to get past, so timing

is essential. When you get about halfway down (12) you must bounce up onto a box platform and use a series of bounce pads to reach the wooden walkway at the end, where you find a bomb (13) with a sizzling fuse. (If you fall off any of the boxes you must go back and start over.)

Now work your way through the short maze—again, watch out for impaling spears—to the bounce pad on the ground **(14)**. Use that pad to bounce up onto the adjacent block, then bounce from pad to pad until you reach the control button **(15)** over in the corner. Step on that button to lower four blocks along the route.

Now walk back to the bomb **(13)**. When you pick it up, its detonation timer starts counting down from 11! Hurry! Carry the bomb down the lane you just cleared when you lowered the four blocks. When you reach the bounce pad **(14)** on the ground again (see the screenshot) immediately use it to bounce up onto the platform to the left. Quickly push the control stick shown onscreen to toss the bomb at the barricade **(16)**.

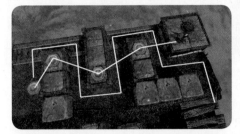

BOMB, BOMB AGAIN

If your first attempt to bomb the barricade fails, don't worry—a new bomb spawns back at (13) the moment the previous one explodes. Just go back, grab the new bomb, and try another run.

Once you blast open the barricade, use the series of bounce pads to hop across boxes (timing your leaps to miss the impaling spears) and reach the hatbox **(17)**. Shake out the Fancy Hat.

Now you can hop down to the whirlwind below and use it to exit the Sky Ramparts. Switch back to your Magic Skylander and return to The Battlement.

FINISH REBUILDING THE BRIDGE

Work your way down the battlement walkway, fighting past guards, avoiding the impaling spears, and lowering the lightning pylons at **(18)** and **(19)** to open gates. Again, each time you lower a pylon, another part of the stronghold bridge is repaired. Watch out for sneaky Chompies hiding inside barrels!

Be ready for a Drow ambush when you reach the last pylon. After you clear the area, shake the Treasure Chest then take the nearby teleport pad **(20)** over to a small island to find a legendary treasure, the Ancient Carillon. Grab it and teleport right back, then lower the last pylon **(19)** to complete the bridge rebuilding.

STORM THE KEEP!

Go to the left and cross the span to reach the stronghold's Inner Keep and face a brand new foe: the Windbag Djinni. This roaring sprite has a nasty ranged attack, firing bolts of lightning at your Skylander. Try to hit the Djinni from outside its range, or wait until right after its lightning attack fades, rush in for quick attacks, and then duck back out of range.

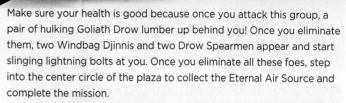

NEW AREA FOUND
"INNER KEEP" (AIR)

BEAT THE GEM CLOCK

Follow the circular stone curving up the keep. Several lethal Drow Witches are posted on the battlements. A Soul Gem **(22)** is stashed behind a barred gate on the left—ignore it for now and continue around the walkway. Eventually you reach an area with a big door and a floor switch **(21)**. Fight off the ambush then approach the switch (circled in the screenshot).

When you step on floor switch you see a quick cinematic of the Soul Gem gate bars dropping. Now you must sprint back down the walkway through the obstacle course of noxious plants as you try to reach the gem before the gate rises again! (You can retry this as many times as necessary.)

A countdown timer shows you how much time you have left. When you beat the clock for the gem, you unlock the "Thick Shelled" power for the Air Skylander named Warnado.

FIND THE ETERNAL AIR SOURCE

Go back up the spiraling walkway past the big door. Run up the long stretch of impaling spear sections, timing your run to avoid injury. Continue up to the top plaza where

an Air Spell Punk casts protection on a trio of Drow Witches posted directly underneath the Eternal Air Source.

Make sure your health is good because once you attack this group, a pair of hulking Goliath Drow lumber up behind you! Once you eliminate them, two Windbag Djinnis and two Drow Spearmen appear and start slinging lightning bolts at you. Once you eliminate all these foes, step into the center circle of the plaza to collect the Eternal Air Source and complete the mission.

BACK AT THE RUINS: THE LOCK PUZZLE

Watch as the Eternal Air Source gets integrated into the Core, and Kaos laments over your success. Hugo suggests that you investigate the ruckus at the docks while he figures out your next step.

Head down the staircase to the dock area. Your arrival triggers a scene: an imprisoned fish-like fellow named Gurglefin asks for help. Approach the Lockmaster Imp at the lock to bring up the Lock Puzzle mini-game. Your goal is to rotate the lock so the imp slides through all the tumblers, the pink glowing disks. Doing so unlocks the Lock Puzzle.

This one's not too tough. Turn the Lock Puzzle R, L, L, R, and R to unlock the box. This triggers another scene: Gurglefin asks for help against the trolls on his home island who have enslaved his people.

5

OILSPILL ISLAND

Find Gurglefin the Gilman at the docks below the Ruins and agree to shove off for Oilspill Island in his ship. You arrive on Tadpole Island and learn that a troll oil-drilling operation has befouled the place. The trolls have enslaved Gurglefin's fish people as well. Your job: Set them free then destroy the oil refinery.

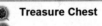

	**Treasure Chest**
	Hat
	Soul Gem
	Story Scroll
	Legendary Item
——	Direct path from Start to Goal
——	Optional paths for bonus items

NEW AREA FOUND
"TADPOLE ISLAND"

OBJECTIVES
FREE THE CAGED GILMEN (5 TOTAL)
DESTROY THE TROLL REFINERY

ELEMENTAL GATES
FIRE

AREAS TO FIND
TADPOLE ISLAND
ACCESS PLATFORM ALPHA
SLUDGE MARSH
ACCESS PLATFORM BETA
DRILL PLATFORM DELTA
THE REFINERY
EXHAUST VENT ZETA

NEW ENEMIES

TROLL GREASEMONKEY

TECH SPELL PUNK

BLASTER TROLL

TROLL GRENADIER

MARK 31 TROLL TANK

COLLECTIONS

SOUL GEMS

Carapace Plating
(Wham-Shell)

Troll Bomb Boot
(Boomer)

LEGENDARY TREASURE

Catechumen

HATS

Plunger Head

STORY SCROLLS

From Tonic to Toxic

Originally, oil was a popular hair tonic for Molekin. Unfortunately it made all their hair fall out. Now that the Molekin are all bald, Oil is pretty much just used as a fuel source for tech machines.

From Tonic to Toxic

MISSION GUIDE

After you arrive, cross the island to the left and pick up the Story Scroll—"From Tonic to Toxic"—tucked behind the hut. Follow the dock to the next zone, Access Platform Alpha.

NEW AREA FOUND

"ACCESS PLATFORM ALPHA"

BEAM OPEN THE FIRST GATE

This triggers your first meeting with a Troll Greasemonkey **(1)**. These ornery fellows swing a mean wrench at close range, so keep your distance and nail them with ranged fire if you can.

LOOTING

Don't forget to smash the pipes and other materials stacked on the various islands and platforms. The items that drop are worth gold!

Move onto the access platform. Your next task is to redirect the pink energy beam to open the gate. To do so, simply push the movable crystal forward twice so it catches the energy beam and shoots it into the gate mechanism, powering it up.

FIND THE SOUL GEM

Before you move on, descend the stairs on the platform's right side **(2)** to Sludge Marsh, where the Tech element is strongest. To glide across water you need either a Water Skylander or any flying Skylander. (With upgrades, Spyro or Sonic Boom can fly, but your best option is a flying Tech Skylander like Drobot.)

NEW AREA FOUND

"SLUDGE MARSH" (TECH)

Blast through all the debris and dead fish (some drop treasure) to the Soul Gem hovering next to the pipeline. This Soul Gem unlocks the "Carapace Plating" power for the Water Skylander named Wham Shell.

FIND THE DRILL PLATFORM

Now you can either return to the first platform and go through the gate you just opened; or you can simply glide over the water to the pier that leads up to the next zone **(3)**, Access Platform Beta, where the Water element is strongest.

NEW AREA FOUND
"ACCESS PLATFORM BETA" (WATER)

There you encounter your first Tech Spell Punk. This foe calls down deadly tracking lasers from above. The spell starts out blue and tracks your Skylander, but when it turns red it locks

into place on the ground, marking where the next blasts will arrive. If you see these red glyphs near you, move away quickly! Two more Troll Greasemonkeys waddle into the fray too, so keep moving and launching your attacks from range.

Clearing the area opens a gate at the top of the next ramp. Climb the ramp and use the bounce pad to reach the Treasure Chest on the metal platform to the left. Bounce

back and proceed down the wooden walkway until you meet another new Troll enemy, the Troll Blaster **(4)**. This gun-wielding grunt is slow on the draw—his gun glows green as he raises it, then he aims for a long second before pulling the trigger.

Blast him before he gets off his powerful shot, which once fired is almost impossible to dodge. Proceed into the next zone, Drill Platform Delta, and consider switching to a Tech Skylander because the Tech element is stronger here.

NEW AREA FOUND
"DRILL PLATFORM DELTA" (TECH)

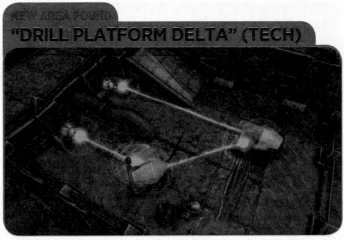

FREE THE CAGED GILMEN

Now you reach another energy beam puzzle. To open the next gate you must redirect the pink beam so it shoots into the gate crystal next to the ramp. First, push the movable crystal all the way forward. Next, use the nearby lever to turn the energy beam until it hits the crystal you pushed, which reflects the beam into the gate crystal to lower the gate. (See the screenshot for the final arrangement.)

Head up the ramp through the lowered gate onto the drill platform to find a key, a prisoner in a cage, a new foe, and another energy beam puzzle. This area leads to good deal of stuff. First, grab the key and use it to liberate the Gilman from the cage **(5)**.

Second, smash through the wooden fence just past the cage, turn left, and approach the staircase descending into the Sludge Marsh. Switch to a flying or Water

Skylander (if you aren't one already) and glide around the pipe to the Soul Gem **(6)** floating above the water. (This one unlocks the "Troll Bomb Boot" power for the Tech Skylander, Boomer.) Glide back to the staircase and climb out of the water.

Third, find the wooden walkway on the left and follow it to the Treasure Chest at the end. Now return to the crystals on the drill platform.

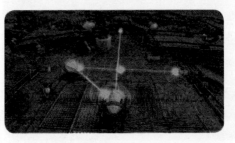

Push the movable crystal once toward the camera and once to the left. Use the nearby lever three times to redirect the pink beam into the crystal you just moved; this opens the next gate. (See the screenshot for the final alignment.)

BEAM THE BAD GUYS

Pink energy beams can take out Trolls. Rotate the beam through enemy locations to eliminate them!

Approach the newly opened gate warily—three Troll Greasemonkeys rush out and a new foe, the Troll Grenadier, tosses his grenades down from his high perch. Wipe out the Greasemonkeys and go through the gate where three more Grenadiers guard another poor caged Gilman **(7)**.

Dodge the bombs and eliminate the Grenadiers! (You can also take out Trolls by rotating the energy beam through them.) Grab the nearby key and unlock the fish guy's prison—that's two Gilmen freed, with three more to go. Rotate the energy beam so it hits the gate crystal next to the ramp. This opens the gate **(8)** into the next area.

Go through that newly opened gate and turn left up the metal ramp to find another key **(9)**. Take it back down the ramp to free the third caged Gilman **(10)**. Just two more to go now! Now the climb the metal ramp again and turn right to the elemental gate sphere **(11)**.

ELEMENTAL GATE: FIRE

Switch to a Fire Skylander such as Ignitor, Eruptor or Flameslinger. Unlock the elemental gate and step into the flaming refinery pipe **(12)** just beyond. This shoots you through the pipes into a new zone, The Refinery.

NEW AREA FOUND
"THE REFINERY" (FIRE)

FIND THE HAT

You end up on a small platform with three pipes **(13)**. The Refinery is a crazy maze of pipes connecting a network of platforms, and it's easy to lose your bearings here. Two special items, a hat and a legendary treasure, are stashed on two of the platforms.

First, step into the leftmost exit pipe to travel to another platform with two pipes **(14)**. Here, step into the leftmost pipe again to travel to a circular platform **(15)** with a hatbox. Shake open the hatbox to acquire the Plunger Head. Wearing it gives you a nice power boost and makes an excellent fashion statement as well.

FIND THE LEGENDARY TREASURE

Leave the hatbox platform via the left exit pipe. This takes you to platform **(16)**. Take the right pipe exit to reach platform **(17)**. Next, take the left pipe exit to travel to platform **(18)** where you see a lever. Pull the lever to see the center pipe open up, clear back at **(13)**!

Leave the lever platform via the only pipe exit to reach platform **(19)**. Use the bounce pad here to score some floating treasure! Exit that platform via the left pipe to reach platform **(20)** and scoop up more treasure. Exit via the rightmost pipe to return to platform **(13)**.

Here you can use that newly opened center pipe to travel all the way to **(21)** where you can finally grab a legendary treasure, the Catechumen. From this platform, the only pipe exit transports your Skylander out of The Refinery, just outside the elemental gate.

FREE THE FOURTH GILMAN

From the plateau where you freed the third Gilman **(10)** fight up the ramp and wipe out a veritable army of Trolls (including Greasemonkeys, Blasters, and Grenadiers) guarding a teleport pad **(22)**, circled in the screenshot. When the way is clear, step onto the pad.

This zaps you to another platform **(23)** where a Tech Spell Punk starts dropping lasers on you! Blast through the barrels and grab the key, run up the ramp to eliminate the Punk, then open the cage to liberate the fourth Gilman. Only one left! Use the teleport pad to cross over the gap to **(25)**.

FREE THE FIFTH GILMAN

Fight off the pair of Troll Blasters that meet you. Turn your attention to the big Mark 31 Troll Tank that defends both the final cage and its key. Destroy it, but don't relax when it explodes! A Troll Greasemonkey hops out, seeking revenge for losing his lovely tank. Once you take out the Troll, grab the key and unlock the cage to free the final Gilman.

DESTROY THE REFINERY

Gurglefin is grateful, but he has one more request. The Troll factory is polluting the waters around where the Gilmen live. He asks if you'll destroy it with one of the bombs floating nearby **(27)**. After the scene you end up on a ramp. First, go nab the Treasure Chest to the right, guarded by a single Tech Spell Punk. Grab a bomb, run it to the big smoke belcher, and toss it over one last Punk into the stack to complete the mission.

NEW AREA FOUND
"EXHAUST VENT ZETA" (TECH)

BACK AT THE RUINS: OIL THE FAR VIEWER

Afterwards, Gurglefin presents his gift of an "oil donkey." Coincidentally, Hugo needs oil for the Far Viewer, which is rusted and won't turn. Grab the oilcan on the dock and bring it upstairs to the Far Viewer. Use the control shown onscreen to oil the telescope. Now Hugo can spot the next item you need for the Core of Light: the Twin Spouts of Ocea-Major-Minor. Unfortunately, they're stashed in a pirate-infested hangout called Dark Water Cove.

BUTTERFLY BARGAINS

Look for the blue butterfly called the Winged Sapphire next to Persephone's podium. Catch it to earn a 2 percent discount whenever you buy upgrades from the fairy. Keep an eye out for these creatures between missions! You can collect up to 10 of them in the game.

6

Find Gurglefin by his boat at the docks and agree to sail to Dark Water Cove. When you arrive at the eerie cove, the main gates are closed so Gurglefin docks at the outer island. To find the Twin Spouts you must first reconnoiter a way into the fortress.

DARK WATER COVE

GOAL

START

Legend

 Treasure Chest

 Hat

 Soul Gem

 Story Scroll

 Legendary Item

— Direct path from Start to Goal

— Optional paths for bonus items

OBJECTIVES

FIND THE TWIN SPOUTS' LOCATION

RETRIEVE THE TWIN SPOUTS

ESCAPE IN THE PIRATE SHIP

ELEMENTAL GATES

MAGIC

WATER

AREAS TO FIND

THE NORTH STAR

BATTERY ISLAND

WHALE'S BELLY

EAST GATE

LOST RIGGER'S COVE

TORTA'S TOWN

BRIDGE OF HANDS

THE ANCIENT TEMPLE

THE ELVENSHIP

WEST GATE

WATERY GRAVES

NEW ENEMIES

NAUTELOID

BLASTANEER

SQUIDFACE BRUTE

WATER SPELL PUNK

SQUIDDLER

COLLECTIONS

SOUL GEMS

**Sticky Boomerangs
(Dino-Rang)**

**Fire Forged Armor
(Ignitor)**

LEGENDARY TREASURE

Parrot Totem

HATS

Tiki Hat

Tropical Turban

STORY SCROLLS

Pirate Problems

A note from a salty reading says,
"It's not easy being a Pirate. Many
complain of long hours, sea sickness
and parrot bites. Worst of all is
having to explain what a poop deck
is."

Pirate Problems

MISSION GUIDE

Start by heading up the gangway to the left and boarding the pirate ship, The North Star. Blast all the cannons and other stuff on the deck to release valuable treasures, and then grab the Soul Gem. (It unlocks the "Sticky Boomerangs" power for the Earth Skylander, Dino-Rang.)

NEW AREA FOUND
"THE NORTH STAR"

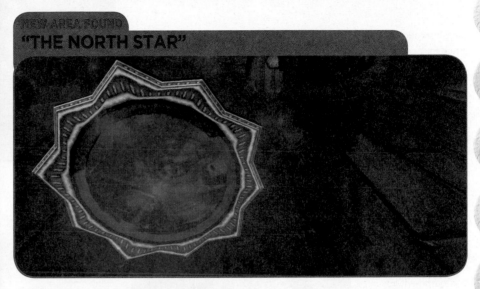

SILENCE THE ARTILLERY

Exit the ship and proceed past Gurglefin up the long dock. Suddenly, the pirate artillery battery spots you and opens fire. Its very first shot sinks Gurglefin's boat! The cannon **(2)** is located atop a high hill on the island up ahead.

   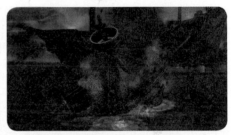

As you move forward onto Battery Island, the cannon's "aiming reticle" appears on the ground, tracking your Skylander. If one of these yellow markers catches up to your character, it locks onto the location, turns into a red crosshairs, and then a cannonball hits the spot and explodes. Keep moving to avoid taking damage. The artillery will continue to target you until you can eliminate it.

NEW AREA FOUND
"BATTERY ISLAND" (EARTH)

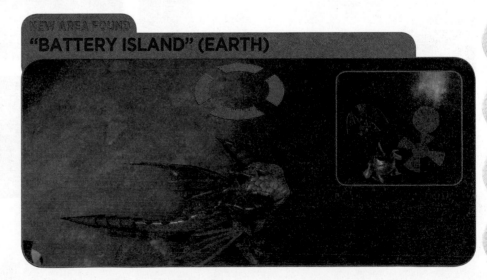

PIRATE BOOTY

Pirates steal good loot and stash it everywhere, so smash all the breakable objects you find.

Smash through the stone barricades to face a new enemy, the nasty little Nauteloid **(1)**. These beasts make quick, beeline dashes at you with their serrated, razor-sharp snouts. Try to nail them before they can get close.

Keep working your way uphill to the artillery so you can terminate the relentless bombardment. En route you encounter another new foe, the Blastaneer.

This pirate hauls a mini-cannon that fires two painful blasts in quick succession. He's slow to reload, however, so dodge the first two shots then hit the Blastaneer fast and hard before he can fire again.

When you finally reach the cannon **(2)** and its cannoneer, eliminate them and cross the gangway onto the next pirate ship, Whale's Belly **(3)**.

NEW AREA FOUND
"WHALE'S BELLY"

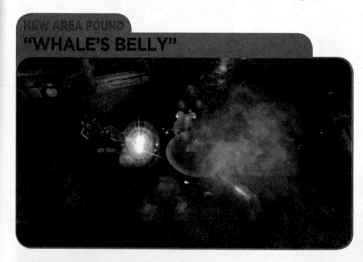

FIND THE ELEMENTAL GATE

Bounce up to the crow's nest on the mast and walk carefully along the plank so you can drop to the raised aft deck. Approach the raised gangway; it slowly lowers to allow your exit onto the East Gate docks, a zone where the Water element is strongest. But two Blastaneers block your path, so be ready for a fight!

NEW AREA FOUND
"EAST GATE" (WATER)

Climb the stairs at the end of the dock and bash through the wooden gate to acquire the key. When you do, a quick zooming cinematic shows you another locked gate

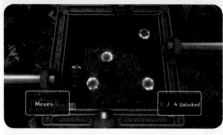

(9) on the far side of the island. For now, use the key in hand to open the nearby East Gate exit. Fight your way past more Nauteloids and Blastaneers to the gate with a Lock Puzzle.

Solve the lock puzzle by turning the Lock Puzzle as follows: 4L, 2R, L, 4R, 2L. This gives you a perfect score of 13 moves. For the Wii, the solution is: 4R, 2L, R. When the gate opens, step through and turn right before you reach the bridge. Veer left off of the grassy slope so you drop down to a beach area with a bounce pad. Using a flying or Water Skylander, glide directly across the water to the Story Scroll (circled in the screenshot) entitled "Pirate Problems" glowing on the opposite beach.

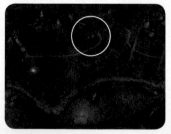 

Cross back to the beach and use the bounce pad to hop back up onto the grassy slope. Climb toward the right to the elemental gate.

ELEMENTAL GATE: MAGIC

Use a Magic Skylander like Spyro to unlock the gate and proceed into a new zone, Lost Rigger's Cove, strong in the Magic element. Follow the wooden walkway to the boarded-in cave **(5)** and smash it open to reveal a teleport pad. Step onto the pad to transport across the cove to the base of the tall waterfall **(6)** (circled in the screenshot).

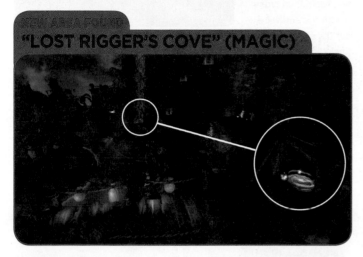

NEW AREA FOUND
"LOST RIGGER'S COVE" (MAGIC)

Clear out the hostiles from the area, including a new foe, the lumbering Squidface Brute. The Brute swings a sharp anchor, but it sticks in the ground if he misses, giving you time to get in a few good shots before he recovers. After the fight, use the bounce pads to hop up the cliff platforms to the Lock Puzzle.

Solve the lock puzzle by turning the Lock Puzzle as follows:
3L, 5R, 2L, 2R, 2L.

When the gate opens, enter and shake open the hatbox inside to acquire the Tiki Hat which boosts the wearer's Elemental Power by a whopping +10. Don the hat if you want. Step carefully off the left side of the cliff platform to drop to a lower platform loaded with treasure. Drop from the right side of that platform to the ground next to the teleport pad where you started. Now you can exit Rigger's Cove back into the East Gate area.

FIND THE TWIN SPOUTS

Cross the stone bridge to face another Squidface Brute **(7)**. Defeat him and drop down to the small beach on the left to snag a Treasure Chest. Use the bounce pad next to it to hop back up to the path.

Cross the next stone bridge to face yet another new foe, the Water Spell Punk. This Punk calls down damaging spells from above—in this case, freezing water puddles. Avoid the circular puddles on the ground. Any Skylander caught in one gets frozen inside a rising block of ice, forcing you to jiggle the control shown onscreen to break out!

PUNK FREEZE

The freezing water puddles called down the Water Spell Punk don't inflict direct damage, but they freeze your Skylander in a block of ice if you step into them. Jiggle the control shown onscreen to escape a freeze!

Keep following the path over another bridge to Torta's Town **(8)**, strong in the Earth element. Look out! Another battery of artillery spots your Skylander and opens fire, so dodge the yellow targeting reticles again. Hop down to the beach on the right to collect another Soul Gem (circled in the screenshot). This one unlocks the "Fire Forged Armor" power for Ignitor. Use the nearby bounce pad to hop back up to the main path and follow it up into town.

NEW AREA FOUND
"TORTA'S TOWN" (EARTH)

Fight through the Blastaneers in town. Look for a key in the main square, but leave it for now. First, blast through the barrels blocking the entrance to the large building (circled in the screenshot) at the left end of town. Enter and step onto the teleport pad to zap up to the plateau to the right of town. Follow the plateau around to the legendary treasure, the Parrot Totem.

When you enter the temple, its entry doors slam shut and you face an ambush. Take out the attackers in the first room then cross the bridge and wipe out the attackers (including another Water Spell Punk) guarding the Twin Spouts **(11)**. Climb the steps and acquire the Twin Spouts to trigger a short scene: Gurglefin congratulates you, but now you must steal a pirate frigate to escape.

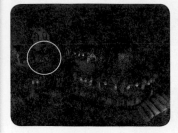 

Go left and drop from the plateau. Grab the key in the town square if you haven't already done so then head back to the right. Proceed all the way past the walkway and the "boathouse" to the ornate gate. Use the key to unlock the gate. Behind it is a Water Spell Punk guarding the entry to the Bridge of Hands. Blast him!

OPEN THE MAIN GATE

After the scene, you end up back across the island **(12)**. Although your primary goal is to reach the frigate, you still have three special treasures to collect, if you want. Fight down the wooden walkway to the next ship, The Elvenship **(13)**. Once you clear the way, Gurglefin reports that you must open the main gate in order to escape! The gate switch is atop the nearby watchtower, your final Goal.

NEW AREA FOUND
"BRIDGE OF HANDS"

NEW AREA FOUND
"THE ELVENSHIP" (WATER)

COLLECT THE TWIN SPOUTS

Proceed across the bridge to face your first Squiddler who shoots explosive blowfish at you. These spiky menaces track you then glow red and explode, but you can blast them before they detonate. Continue up the bridge to The Ancient Temple **(10)**, where Magic is the strong element.

The next steps are fun. Aboard The Elvenship, climb the stairs to the bounce pad and use it to leap up to the crow's next atop the main mast. Walk carefully across the plank to the row of gems and follow them until you drop down onto another bounce pad. Use that pad to bound across to the balcony where you find a teleport pad **(14)** in a cave.

NEW AREA FOUND
"THE ANCIENT TEMPLE" (MAGIC)

NEW AREA FOUND
"WEST GATE"

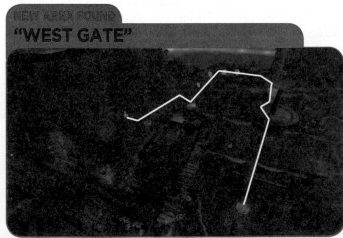

Use the teleport to zap over to a plateau where you score a nice Treasure Chest. Then use the teleport pad there to return to the balcony. Use the bounce pad to jump down to the ground, then head right to the elemental gate.

ELEMENTAL GATE: WATER

Use a Water Skylander to unlock the gate and then walk right into the whirlpool just beyond it. You emerge in a new zone called Watery Graves, strong in the Water element. Use a Water Skylander to cross over to the opposite bank and use the bounce pad to hop up the cliff and find another Treasure Chest.

NEW AREA FOUND
"WATERY GRAVES" (WATER)

Now ride the moving rafts from platform to platform until you reach the raft with a bounce pad **(16)**. Use it to hop over to the stationary platform with a bounce pad, and use that pad in turn to hop up onto the wooden platform above the waterfall.

From there you can ride the next moving raft over to the platform holding a hatbox. Shake open the hatbox to acquire the Tropical Turban then use the teleport pad to transport back to the whirlpool. Use it to exit the Watery Graves area back into West Gate.

OPEN THE MAIN GATE

Now you can smash through the wooden gate and defeat the pair of Squidface Brutes to reach the watchtower stairs. Climb up to the gate switch and press the control shown onscreen to lower the gate and complete the mission by escaping on the pirate frigate. Watch as the Twin Spouts of Ocea-Major-Minor are installed in the Core of Light and Hugo explains how to acquire the Eternal Water Source, and warns about the dreaded Leviathan.

7

LEVIATHAN LAGOON

Treasure Chest

Hat

Soul Gem

Story Scroll

Legendary Item

— Direct path from Start to Goal

— Optional paths for bonus items

Find Gurglefin by the dock and agree to sail off to Leviathan Lagoon. You arrive just in time to see a rather large fish leap from the water and wreak some havoc. Pirates have beaten you to the lagoon. So now the race for the Eternal Water Source is on!

GOAL

START

OBJECTIVES

BRING 4 STATUES TO THE SHRINE

FIND THE ETERNAL WATER SOURCE

ELEMENTAL GATES

WATER

AREAS TO FIND

PEARL CLUSTER

PLANK WALK

TURTLE ISLAND

SHARK'S TOOTH ISLAND

THE SHRINE

NEW ENEMIES

HOB 'N' YARO

DARK WATER DRAGON

DARK ICE YETI

DARK AMPHIBIOUS GILLMAN

MISSION GUIDE

Four statues are scattered around the island chain. As Gurglefish explains, you must find all four and place them in the Shrine before the Water Source will reveal itself. Cross the bridge into the Pearl Cluster zone where you spot a larcenous little Hob 'n' Yaro, a new enemy, stealing the first statue!

COLLECTIONS

SOUL GEMS

Love for the Sea (Zap)

LEGENDARY TREASURE

Opulent Pullet

HATS

Napoleon Hat

STORY SCROLLS

Tales of the fish.

A note from Professor P. Grungally says, "For years fishermen have hunted an enormous, hungry fish that lurked in the deep end of the lagoon. No one has seen the fish lately... or the fishermen, come to think of it."

Tales of the fish

NEW AREA FOUND
"PEARL CLUSTER"

Smash through the wooden fence. Watch out for that overturned boat! When you approach it, four Nauteloids pop out from underneath to attack. Wipe them out!

Instead of crossing the next bridge, switch to a Water Skylander and dive into the water moving toward the camera. Swim along the line of rocks until you reach the elemental gate.

MINIMIZE WATER TIME

Whenever your Skylander swims in the waters around Leviathan Lagoon, there's a chance the Leviathan will suddenly appear and gulp your guy whole. You end up inside the Leviathan's mouth!

The longer you're in the water, the greater the chance that this happens, so don't take leisurely swims and keep an eye out for the great fish below. If you get gulped, don't panic— just shoot three times and the big fish spits you out.

Skylanders with a flight ability active aren't in any danger from the Leviathan.

GET THE FIRST STATUE

Hob 'n' Yaros are sneaky, swift, and can be difficult to catch. This fellow runs across the next bridge but gets trapped behind some barrels. Blast him and collect the first statue. This triggers a short cinematic that reveals the second statue's location **(7)**.

ELEMENTAL GATE: WATER

Use your Water Skylander to unlock the gate then enter the whirlpool just beyond in a new zone called Plank Walk—strong in the Water element, unsurprisingly. You pop up in a pool on the next island. Don't use the nearby teleport pad yet. (It zaps you right back to the starting island.) Instead, cross the wooden bridge to reach a triangle of islands.

NEW AREA FOUND
"PLANK WALK" (WATER)

A Treasure Chest sits on the island to the left. There's a hatbox visible as well, but it's in the grimy grips of another Hob 'n' Yaro thief. Fight through the Blastaneers to nab the chest, watching out for the Squiddlers lobbing blowfish at you from the center island (3). Then chase down the thief and blast him to get the hatbox and shake out the Napoleon Hat, a nice reward for your trouble. Return to the teleport pad and use it to leave Plank Walk.

GET THE SECOND STATUE

Follow the island chain walkways to Turtle Island, strong in the Life element. Clear the way up to the three giant turtles (4), push into the gap ahead to form a bridge, and then cross over.

NEW AREA FOUND
"TURTLE ISLAND" (LIFE)

As you cross the bridge toward the next island, a Hob 'n' Yaro pops out of his tent and nabs the key that you need to open the nearby locked gate (5). Proceed to Shark's Tooth Island, strong in the Water element, and grab the Story Scroll to the right entitled "Tales of the Fish."

NEW AREA FOUND
"SHARK'S TOOTH ISLAND" (WATER)

Hob 'n' Yaro is almost impossible to catch as he flees every time you approach. But you can push the giant turtle (6) to the left to block the wooden bridge. Next time you chase the thief around, he gets trapped by the turtle and you can blast him to acquire the key. Use the key to open the gate and proceed.

Cross the next bridge and push the turtle back to clear the way to the next statue (7). Grab the statue—but before you continue on, turn around and push the turtle back into the gap between the walkways. (This allows you to reach the Treasure Chest up on the raised walkway.)

GET THE THIRD STATUE

Move quickly to minimize damage from all the exploding blowfish that the two Squiddlers keep shooting down at you from above. Drop down the ledge and use the nearby teleport pad (revealed after you blast a tent) to zap over to the small island where you can climb the ramp onto the walkway. Now you can finally blast the annoying Squiddlers and grab the chest.

Drop down again and move across Shark's Tooth Island—again, watch out for nasty surprises underneath overturned boats. At the tip of the island follow the narrow gangplank over to a Soul Gem that unlocks the "Love for the Sea" power for the Water Skylander named Zap.

When you cross the next bridge you see another Hob 'n' Yaro speed ahead of you and nab the third statue (8). Like the previous thief, this one is difficult to catch as he sprints around in a circle over the bridges. Once again, push the nearby giant turtle so it blocks the bridge access (9), then run around the opposite way and chase the Hob 'n' Yaro until it's trapped on the bridge against the turtle. Blast the thief, grab the third statue, and move on.

LEGENDARY ITEM!

After you sink the pirate ship, hop into the water and allow Leviathan to scoop up your Skylander. In his mouth you can find the Opulent Pullet, a truly legendary treasure.

Gurglefin waits for you atop the brick tower (10), but first walk around behind it to find the last Treasure Chest (circled in the screenshot). Go back to the stairs and climb up to meet your fish friend.

Gurglefin reports the grim news: the pirates have captured the last statue and are making a run with it! He suggests you use the nearby cannon to sink the escaping pirate ship.

SINK THE PIRATE SHIP!

Hop in the cannon and open fire on the pirate ship. It makes multiple passes back and forth, so don't worry if you don't sink it on the first pass. Target the masts first. Once all three are knocked off, just unload into the hull until the disabled pirate vessel rams into the gap between the next two islands (11).

GET THE FOURTH STATUE

Go to the derelict vessel and grab the final statue. Next, head to the Shrine, a new zone strong in the Magic element. When you reach the glowing disk, step into it to trigger the final sequence: the four statues are placed and the Eternal Water Source rises from the water at the end of the dock! Walk toward the glowing source to trigger a surprising development.

NEW AREA FOUND

"THE SHRINE" (MAGIC)

DEFEAT THE EVIL MINIONS OF KAOS!

Inside Leviathan, your Skylander takes a meeting with Kaos himself. When the scene ends, Kaos unleashes one of his minions, the Dark Water Dragon.

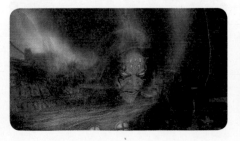

This minion is deadly but beatable, especially if you have upgraded your Skylanders and put hats on them. His attacks mirror Spyro's own, with a dashing Charge and a spitting Waterball attack. Keep moving when you're not launching your own attacks. Your foe's Waterball hits can slow you down, so take special care to avoid them.

When the Dark Water Dragon finally falls, Kaos releases more minions—he calls them "the Deadly Shark Bath of Doomsharks." Waves of toothy sharks start swimming at you in this "bath." You can both dodge and blast them. If a shark hits your Skylander you suffer damage. Keep dodging and blasting sharks until the waves halt.

Next you face Kaos' Dark Amphibious Gillman. This fellow is an evil version of Gill Grunt, with his harpoon attack firing three projectiles at once. Note his attack pattern: before he fires he stops, raises his head and opens his mouth. When you see this behavior, dodge to the side. He fires three quick shots, after which he checks his weapon for a few seconds. Counterattack during this post-shot lull in his attack!

Next, Kaos hits you with another Shark Bath of Doomsharks. Again, blast and dodge sharks until the toothy waves halt. After that he unleashes his Dark Ice Yeti. This four-armed fellow has a nasty melee punch in close, but if you back away he slings an ice spell that juts painful ice crystals up underneath you.

Finally, Kaos unleashes all three minions at once! And if that isn't enough, he throws in another Shark Bath of Doom after awhile. If you manage to survive this ordeal, Kaos finally gives up (for now). Your Skylander collects the Eternal Water Source and completes the mission by returning it to the Core of Light for placement. You see a quick cinematic of the beach access gate as it swings open. Hugo sends you down to investigate the beach area.

INVESTIGATE THE BEACH

Go downstairs to the dock area and grab the oilcan next to the oil pump. Then head to the right, proceeding through the newly opened gate to the beach. Grab the Winged Sapphire when you pass through the gate. Approach the second big robot, the one near the railroad tracks, and use the oilcan on it. The Clam-tron 4000 "awakens" and offers to repay you by mashing up clams into a Pearl.

Clams bounce happily around the beach. Go grab some—just run through them before they burrow back into the sand. When you collect enough clams, the Clam-tron 4000 presses you a "Black Pearl"—actually, a Bomb!

There are two additional Winged Sapphires to collect before you continue the adventure. First, select a Skylander that can cross water. Go into the water off the eastern part of the beach. Swim out to the Bounce Pad there, then bounce up a few times to reach a Winged Sapphire. The other Winged Sapphire is behind the gear door on the beach. Take the oil can to the metal man sitting near the door. After applying the oil to him, the door opens. Enter the door and pick up the Winged Sapphire inside.

Hugo appears with a disturbing report that the Cyclopses have stolen the Crystal Eye, another key piece of the Core of Light. To gain access to the Crystal Eye Castle, grab a bomb, run up the stairs to the right, and use the control shown onscreen to toss the bomb at the blocked gate. Once you blow it open, you meet Diggs the Molekin, your guide to the Crystal Eye Castle.

8

CRYSTAL EYE CASTLE

Talk to Diggs at the cave entrance by the beach and agree to follow him to the Crystal Eye Castle. As you cross the bridge, you see a quick cutscene of the Crystal Eye rolled into a castle keep. Upon arrival, Diggs explains that you must destroy the two Seeing Towers in order to open the big gate where the Eye is stored.

	Treasure Chest
	Hat
	Soul Gem
	Story Scroll
	Legendary Item
—	Direct path from Start to Goal
—	Optional paths for bonus items

OBJECTIVES
DESTROY THE TWO TOWERS
GET THE CRYSTAL EYE

ELEMENTAL GATES
EARTH
UNDEAD

AREAS TO FIND
THE GAUNTLET
OUTER COURTYARD
PUZZLE PIT
SECRET TOWER
EAST TOWER
INNER COURTYARD
WEST TOWER
THE TOWER OF EYES

NEW ENEMIES

TIMIDCLOPS

CRUNCHER

CYCLOPS CHOPPER

CYCLOPS CHUCKER

CYCLOPS MAMMOTH

MISSION GUIDE

Hit the eye switch with any attack to open the first gate. An onscreen timer gives you 8 seconds to get through the open gate. Once you do, Diggs starts to tell you something "very important" but a rolling barrel-bomb knocks him off the ramp!

COLLECTIONS

SOUL GEMS

Shard Soul Prison (Prism Break)

LEGENDARY TREASURE

Teddy Cyclops

HATS

Trojan Helmet

Eye Hat

STORY SCROLLS

Stone masons

A note from Professor P. Grungally says, "Cyclopses are amazing stone masons. They've constructed stone castles, statues and temples throughout the Skylands. The stone carved ships of the Cyclops Navy were not their proudest moment."

Stone Masons

CLIMB THE GAUNTLET RAMPS

This first zone, strong in the Earth element, is called The Gauntlet, and it's easy to see why. More explosive barrels start rolling down the ramp, pushed by a pair of one-eyed Timidclopses at the top **(1)**. Dodge the barrels as you climb up to smite the pushers.

NEW AREA FOUND

"THE GAUNTLET" (EARTH)

From the top of the next ramp **(2)**, two more Timidclops push barrels down at you. When you reach them, some vicious Crunchers—tenacious little cousins of the Chompie—sink their teeth into you and won't let go! Jiggle the control stick shown onscreen to shake them loose, and then wipe them out.

Dodge barrels as you climb to the top of the third ramp to face a Cyclops Chopper, an ax-wielding whirling dervish who is invulnerable while spinning. Stay back while he twirls his blade, and then attack immediately after the spinning stops.

The next gate **(3)** has two eye switches. You must strike both to open the gate. Hurry! You have only 4 seconds after you hit the first eye before it deactivates. Now enter a new zone, the Outer Courtyard, strong in the Air element.

"OUTER COURTYARD" (AIR)

Turn left to see a Story Scroll and a new foe, the Cyclops Chucker (4), hurling boulders at you from a platform. Several spinning Choppers rush at you as well. Clear the area and grab the scroll, entitled "Stone Masons." Don't leave before you climb the stairs (5) on the right and blast the plain-looking cart. Hidden inside is a

legendary treasure, the Teddy Cyclops. Strike the eye switch and run to get through the gate before time runs out.

MAKE TURTLE BRIDGES

The next area features another fun turtle-pushing puzzle. First, clear the area of Cruncher-filled barrels. Push the first two turtles into the floor gap (6) then cross over them and push the third turtle into the next room. Walk around that third turtle and push him back twice so he forms a bridge with the walkway above.

Climb the stairs and cross over the stacked turtles to push the next turtle to the left so he falls to the floor. You can now reach the next staircase. But before you climb, push the fifth turtle away from the camera twice so he forms a bridge on the next level up. Now you can climb the stairs and continue on.

Before you use the nearby elemental gate, continue around the corner to the right (7) and follow the narrow walkway to a Soul Gem. This one unlocks the "Shard

Soul Prison" power for Prism Break. Then continue on to a second elemental gate (8) just to the right.

ELEMENTAL GATE: EARTH

Use an Earth Skylander to unlock the gate and cross the bridge to a platform with a teleport pad. Step on the pad to reach the Puzzle Pit (9). This block puzzle can be tricky.

"PUZZLE PIT" (EARTH)

Your ultimate goal is to rearrange the blocks so you can reach the circular platform on the opposite side (12) where you can find a hatbox and use the teleport pad there to return to the castle.

An extra bonus goal is to use the eye switch on the right-side platform (10) to open the gate on the left-side platform (11) then beat the timer to the open gate so you can reach the Treasure Chest there.

Here's how the puzzle mechanism works:

- Each block in the 7-by-7-block Puzzle Pit can be in one of two positions, up or down.
- Blocks rise and fall in different combinations whenever you step on one of the seven circular floor pads—three pads on each side and one in the center of the puzzle.
- When you stand next to a floor pad, the blocks that turn yellow are the ones that will reverse position (rise or fall) when you step on that pad.
- Each floor pad moves the same block combination every time you step on it. So if you step on any pad two times in a row (i.e., without stepping on any other pad in between), the second step simply reverses the block movement of the first step. In other words, you can "take back" a move by just stepping on the same floor pad again.
- Note that it's possible to slip around a floor pad without activating it—just walk around the edge of the block. But if you accidentally click a pad that you didn't want to click, just step on the pad again to reverse the blocks you just moved.

It sounds complicated, but it's easier than it looks. If you keep running from pad to pad, you can probably get through eventually. Or you can just follow the solution route using the numbers on the screenshots. Step on pads in the following order to get through quickly and acquire both a Treasure Chest and a new hat.

- **This shot shows the puzzle's start configuration.** Step on the floor pads in order from 1 to 6 to reach the eye switch at (10) and create a straight route through the blocks over to the gate (11).

- **Then hit the eye switch and run left without clicking any floor pads** (run around the pads) and hurry through the gate to get the Treasure Chest.

- **This shot shows the puzzle after you've completed the first steps listed above.** Step on the floor pads in order from 1 to 5 to reach the platform with the hatbox and the teleport pad (12).

- **Shake open the hatbox to get the Trojan Helmet** with +10 Armor for better protection during your encounters! Then use the teleport pad to exit the Puzzle Pit.

ELEMENTAL GATE: UNDEAD

Now head up the walkway to the other elemental gate (13). Use an Undead Skylander to unlock this gate and proceed across the bridge to the teleport pad. Use it to reach a small platform (14) with a gate and another teleport pad. (This pad zaps you right back to the elemental gate, so don't use it yet.) Take a breath and prepare for some brutal combat. Hit both eye switches and hurry through the gate to yet another teleport pad (15) and use it to reach the Secret Tower.

NEW AREA FOUND
"SECRET TOWER" (UNDEAD)

As the screenshot reveals in a frightening overview, your Skylander drops into a menacing combat arena filled with foes and hazards. You must eliminate Cruncher-spewing plants while you fend off boulder-tossing Chuckers, a pair of hulking blue Cyclops Mammoth, and a few spinning Choppers, all while avoiding the impaling spears jutting up rhythmically from four sections of the floor. Ouch!

Once you clear the room, shake open the hatbox to get the Eye Hat and use the teleport pad (16) to exit the Secret Tower. Go back through the elemental gate (13) and halt.

DESTROY THE FIRST SEEING TOWER

Whack the nearby eye switch then run left and hit the second eye switch to open the gate. Hurry through and approach the East Tower (14), strong in the Tech element. Its doors open automatically.

Switch to a Tech Skylander like Trigger Happy and clear the arena, which includes a bunch of toothy Crunchers, a few spinning Choppers, and a huge Cyclops Mammoth. The Mammoth likes to launch big lumbering leaps that land with damaging force. Keep your distance and nail him from afar!

NEW AREA FOUND
"EAST TOWER" (TECH)

Blast all four eye beams feeding energy to the main pylon, then blast the pylon itself to destroy the Seeing Tower. Nice work! One tower down, one more to go! Return to the Outer Courtyard.

DESTROY THE SECOND SEEING TOWER

Follow the walkway left until you reach the wide Inner Courtyard **(15)** where another big Mammoth and a few other Cyclops foes await your arrival. Don't miss the Treasure Chest in the corner of the courtyard.

NEW AREA FOUND
"INNER COURTYARD"

Continue on to the collapsed section of walkway **(16)** and drop down into the next area, which is once again part of the Outer Courtyard. Fight your way downstairs, climb the opposite staircase to nab another Treasure Chest, and then continue down to the third staircase.

Look at the overhead shot. You must hit the four eye switches (clrcled in the shot) in order to open the gate **(17)** that leads to the second Seeing Tower. When you hit the first switch a timer starts counting down from 8 seconds. However, each time you hit another switch, the timer resets to 8, so you can nail all four switches fairly easily.

The problem is that two hostile Cyclops Chuckers dog your every step by heaving boulders from the walkway next to the fourth eye switch. You may want to eliminate them before you try your switch-whacking run to the gate. When you get through the gate, approach the West Tower **(18)** and enter the doors that automatically open.

NEW AREA FOUND
"WEST TOWER" (TECH)

Clear the room of Cyclopses. Chuckers tossing rocks are posted atop three podiums where you can't hit them. But you can blast the podiums to smithereens, knocking the Chuckers to the floor where you can blast them too. Once again, destroy all the eye beams feeding energy to the main pylon then blast the pylon itself to destroy the tower. With both Seeing Towers down, the main gate opens.

GET THE CRYSTAL EYE!

Now head up to the main gate **(19)**. Climb the slope to the Tower of Eyes, dodging explosive barrels rolled down by the Timidclopses and rocks tossed by Chuckers. Decimate the foes at the top **(20)** and enter the tower arena for one last crazy melee.

NEW AREA FOUND
"THE TOWER OF EYES" (AIR)

Now you must clear the arena in order to lower the spear-gate around the Crystal Eye. This is a tough fight—fresh foes keep pouring into the arena from side doors—so if your current Skylander drops perilously low in health, pull him off the *Portal of Power* and transfer in a fresh

fighter. When you finally clear the arena, go seize the great eye to complete the mission and trigger your return to the Ruins.

Watch as the Crystal Eye is placed in the Core of Light. Hugo reports that the Eternal Earth Source is in a place called Stonetown where the

villagers are keeping it safe. Talk to Diggs to reach Stonetown.

9

STONETOWN

Talk to Diggs down at the entrance to the bridge and agree to follow him to Stonetown. The Molekin leads your Skylander across the Stone Bridge again to the outskirts of the town. The ground is shaking... a humongous, hideous monster called the Stone Golem is destroying the town!

	Treasure Chest
	Hat
	Soul Gem
	Story Scroll
	Legendary Item
—	Direct path from Start to Goal
—	Optional paths for bonus items

GOAL

START

OBJECTIVES
DEFEAT THE STONE GOLEM

ELEMENTAL GATE
LIFE

AREAS TO FIND
MUSHROOM RIDGE
OLD CYCLOPS FORT
BLUE WATER SWAMP
NEW FORTRESS
TOWN OUTSKIRTS
WAYWARD TOWN
RUMBLING RAVINE

NEW ENEMIES

ROCK WALKER   EARTH SPELL PUNK   STONE GOLEM

COLLECTIONS

SOUL GEMS

Zapper Field Deluxe
(Lightning Rod)

Triceratops Honor Guard
(Bash)

LEGENDARY TREASURE

Mono Lisa

HATS

Top Hat

STORY SCROLLS

What makes a Portal Master?

MISSION GUIDE

You start just outside a fortified Cyclops outpost on Mushroom Ridge, a zone strong in the Life element. Slash through the Chompies to reach the Chompy Pod spawning them and exterminate it.

NEW AREA FOUND
"MUSHROOM RIDGE" (LIFE)

BOMB THE BARRICADE

Note the purple bomb icon glowing on the ground in front of the blocked cave to the right. Hit both eye switches quickly to open the fort's gate, and hurry through into the Old Cyclops Fort.

NEW AREA FOUND
"OLD CYCLOPS FORT" (LIFE)

Fight your way to the bomb on the circular platform (2). Grab the bomb and sprint back to the purple bomb icon at the blocked cave. When you get close, use the control shown onscreen to toss the bomb toward the cave to blast it open.

SPEED BOOST

You may need a speed boost to complete the bomb run on time. Outfit your fastest flying Skylander with a Speed-enhancing hat like the Propeller Cap!

Follow the newly opened path up to the ramparts where you can collect the legendary treasure cleverly named the "Mono Lisa." Return to the fort and proceed all the way to the fort's back gate **(3)**.

OPEN THE BACK GATE

Take a peek at the overview screenshot of the gate area. See the two eye switches (circled) sitting atop the watchtowers on either side? You must hit both to open the gate.

First, clear out the guards on the ground to make things easier. Then use the teleport pad to reach one switch. Hit the switch—a 6-second countdown timer begins. Hurry! Drop to the ground and sprint to the second teleport pad so you can zap up and immediately hit the second switch (resetting the timer to 6 seconds again). Drop to the ground again and sprint through the open gate. Good luck!

CROSS THE SWAMP

Switch to a Water Skylander in this new zone, Blue Water Swamp. Before you cross the wooden bridge, find the Treasure Chest hidden around the outside of the Cyclops fort to the right. Then come back, cross the bridge, and fight your way to the stone platform to nab the Story Scroll entitled "What Makes a Portal Master."

"BLUE WATER SWAMP" (WATER)

Cross the next bridge and push the three giant turtles into the water **(4)** so they form a bridge to the next platform. Two annoying Squiddlers lob their explosive blowfish at you as you cross the turtle-bridge, and they're up too high to target on their platforms.

Hustle past them and get ready to face a new foe, the Rock Walker. This nasty fellow vomits molten lava onto nearby targets. The attack is painful, but his range is short, so keep your distance.

After the Rock Walker falls, swim left to the small island. Blast the tent to uncover a Treasure Chest. (Don't use the teleport pad there. It just zaps you back to the stone tower where you got the Story Scroll.) Swim back and grab the key **(5)** up on the next stone platform. Proceed across the next bridge to encounter another new foe, the Earth Spell Punk **(6)**. This Punk's spell endows your nearby enemies with magic armor, making them harder to eliminate.

Fight your way to New Fortress, blast the tent to the left of the fortress entry plaza, and grab the Soul Gem. (This one unlocks the "Zapper Field Deluxe" power for the Air Skylander named Lightning Rod.) Then approach New Fortress and use the key to open the entry gate.

"NEW FORTRESS" (EARTH)

UNLOCK THE NEW FORTRESS EXIT

Inside, the area is strong in the Earth element. The exit gate leading to Stonetown is a short distance to the left, but it's triple-locked: you need three keys to unlock it. (The overhead shot shows you where those keys are located in the fortress.)

Turn right and go to the block puzzle. You can see the first key **(7)** on a raised platform just to the right, but you must work to reach it. Your first goal is to build a block bridge aligned underneath the row of coins spinning in the air.

Push the rightmost block three times to clear a path through. Push the leftmost block once so it's up against the opposite platform. Push the middle block left so it aligns under the spinning coins. Push the first block all the way back (three pushes) to where it started, under the coins. Now you have a three-block bridge connecting the platforms.

But you're not done yet. Push the remaining block three times through the gap so you can reach the stairs in the corner. Before you climb, however, push that same block back twice into the gap to make a one-block bridge. (Check the screenshot to see the final block arrangement.) Now you can go upstairs and cross the blocks to grab the key!

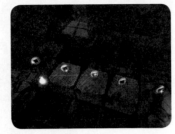

The next key is much easier to acquire. It floats near the exit gate **(8)** so simply grab it and use it on a lock. To get the third key, climb the stairs to the right of the exit gate and follow the corridor until you see the Hob 'n' Yaro steal the key **(9)**. Unfortunately, you can't corner this thief; you must chase and nail him with ranged shots until he drops. (Use your fastest Skylander with a good ranged attack.) Grab the last key and open the New Fortress exit gate.

BLOCK OUT A PATH TO THE SUMMIT

Climb down the back stairs and clear out the enemies on the dirt path. This is brutal combat with Squiddlers, Chompies, and Rock Walkers protected by an Air Spell Punk. Note the

purple bomb icon in front of the barricaded cave entrance **(11)** en route, and the bomb on the podium (circled in the shot) just up ahead.

Continue up the path to the blocks **(10)**. To reach the bomb podium:

- First, go up the ramp on the left and push the block there twice to the right, so it drops into the gap.
- Come back down the ramp and push the first block to the right to form the first part of the bridge to the bomb podium.
- Push the second block back (away from the camera) into the gap to complete the two-block bridge over the gap.
- Go back up the ramp, cross over the newly formed bridge, and push the next block forward twice to finish the bridge to the bomb.

Here's a shot of what the path to the bomb should look like when finished:

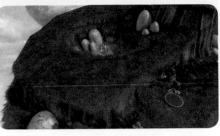

Grab a bomb, sprint back to the cave entrance **(11)**, and toss the bomb to blow open the cave. If the Squiddlers on the two high platforms are harassing you too much, toss bombs up at them first to end the threat before you blast open the cave.

Enter the cave and grab the Soul Gem, which unlocks the "Triceratops Honor Guard" power for the Earth Skylander named Bash. Then return to the blocks at **(10)**.

More Squiddlers firing explosive blowfish make your life miserable here. To make a route up to the top of the hill:

- Climb the ramp, push the next block left twice, then push it back into the narrow gap.
- Climb the next ramp and push each of the next two blocks you encounter into the gap below.
- Push the last block forward twice to get through. Climb the hill and blast the Squiddler menace.
- Go back around to the opposite side of the last block and push it twice again, right back to where it started. This forms the last bridge.

Here's a shot of what the upper path should look like when finished:

When you reach the summit, a quick cinematic plays of the Stone Golem as it crosses the last wooden bridge and punches a poor Stonetown resident. Then the monster stomps into the final clearing **(15)** to await your arrival.

Before you face the golem, however, there is more treasure to be found. Cross the bridge into the Town Outskirts and veer left at the path fork to reach the elemental gate **(12)**.

"TOWN OUTSKIRTS"

ELEMENTAL GATE: LIFE

Switch to a Life Skylander to unlock the gate and proceed across the bridge into the new zone, Wayward Town, strong in the Life element. Take an immediate left and drop down off the broken bridges (see the screenshot) then proceed to sky-island with the bounce pad **(13)**. Use the pad to hop up to the next island with the Treasure Chest.

"WAYWARD TOWN" (LIFE)

Drop off that island at the broken bridge to drop into the town square with six buildings and a bounce pad arranged around a fountain. Use the bounce pad to hop up to the plateau, then use another pad to bounce up to the bomb on a high floating island. Grab the bomb, drop into the town square, and use the explosive to destroy the green-roofed house with coins floating above it (circled in the shot). This reveals a hidden bounce pad **(14)**.

Now it gets tricky. Use the first two bounce pads again to get another bomb. Drop down and use the new bounce pad (revealed by destroying the house) to hop up with the bomb to the blocked cave mouth. Toss the bomb to blast open the cave and reach the hatbox. Shake open the box to collect the Top Hat.

Now you can go back through the elemental gate into the Town Outskirts and proceed up the path into Rumbling Ravine for your meeting with the mighty Stone Golem.

"RUMBLING RAVINE"

DEFEAT THE STONE GOLEM
PHASE 1

The Stone Golem's health bar appears on the right side of the screen. When you keep your distance from the beast, he rolls massive boulders that ricochet back and forth between the ravine's walls—you end up dodging two or three at a time! (The boulders are too big for you to destroy with your attacks.) Sometimes he heaves a rock directly at your Skylander, so be ready to dodge quickly whenever the golem hoists a projectile.

ROCK SHIELD

The gray rock in the center of the Rumbling Ravine arena provides solid protection when the Stone Golem tosses or rolls boulders at you.

If you get too close, the Stone Golem tries to squash you with a vicious foot stomp that radiates damage outward from the point of impact. Your best bet is to hit him from afar with your ranged attacks while keeping an eye on the rolling boulders. When his health drops to 75 percent, he howls and does an angry stomping dance.

PHASE 2

Now the Stone Golem adds in a dangerous new attack: as swirling wind surrounds the monster, he summons down multiple meteors from the sky. Red crosshairs appear on the ground where each new meteor falls, so when you see these, hurry away! Keep using the gray rock as a shield and continue to blast the golem from afar until his health drops to the 50 percent mark.

PHASES 3 AND 4

After another angry stomping dance, the Stone Golem summons meteors again, but this time calls down several at a time, making it hard to dodge them. Keep up your ranged attacks and drop his health further. When it hits the 25 percent mark, he stomps again and summons one more devastating meteor attack. Keep up the pressure, and switch to a fresh Skylander if necessary.

BACK AT THE RUINS

When the Stone Golem finally falls, he drops a ton of loot and the Eternal Earth Source appears in the air. Scoop up the dropped goodies before you step under the Eternal Earth Source to end the mission. Watch as the Core of Light acquires another component—the "eye within the eye"—and a strange new ally named Arbo appears at the Ruins.

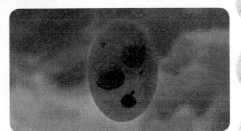

Arbo explains that you must acquire the Life Seeds in order to point the way to the Eternal Life Source. Then the amiable stump calls up a gigantic vine that rises high into the sky. It leads up to Treetop Terrace, the location of the Life Seeds, and thus your next destination!

10 TREETOP TERRACE

Talk to Arbo and agree to climb the vine to the Treetop Terrace. You arrive to discover that the "pointy ears"—the dastardly Drow—have collected the Life Seeds with plans to keep them!

Treasure Chest	
Hat	
Soul Gem	
Story Scroll	
Legendary Item	
——	Direct path from Start to Goal
——	Optional paths for bonus items

OBJECTIVE
COLLECT THE LIFE SEEDS

ELEMENTAL GATES
MAGIC

AREAS TO FIND
THE CANOPY
THE SLUICE GATE
THE HOLLOW
ANCIENT TRUNK
THE SEED TREE

NEW ENEMIES

CORN HORNET

BLADE WITCH

LIFE SPELL PUNK

BLITZER BULLY

MISSION GUIDE

Move forward into the first zone, The Canopy. First thing you meet is a dangerous Corn Hornet that shoots painful stingers that briefly stun your Skylander, but you can swing the controller to regain control quicker. Don't let it get in close where its poison stinger is almost impossible to dodge!

COLLECTIONS

SOUL GEMS

Anchor Cannon
(Gill Grunt)

LEGENDARY TREASURE

Sterling Tapir

HATS

Moose Hat

STORY SCROLLS

History of flight
A note from Professor P. Grungally says, "Despite claims that the Drow invented balloons, it was actually a Chompie who came up with the idea. Drinking two hundred flasks of fizzy juice, a Chompie inflated to twenty times its size and floated away, burping like mad."

History of flight

"THE CANOPY" (AIR)

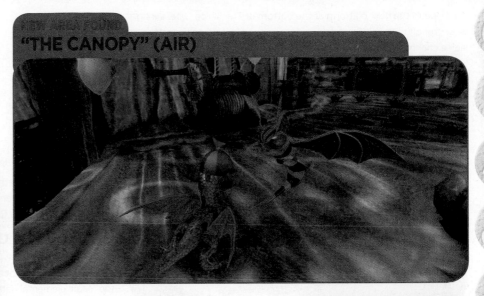

GET PAST THE SLUICE GATE

After you kill the pest, use the winch **(1)** next to the trunk to raise the nearby log gate (circled in the shot). An onscreen timer counts down the time you have before the gate drops again. It's not very far to the gate, but annoying Bounce Pods block the way, so you must slalom through them.

On the next stump you meet a pair of Drow Spearmen plus another new foe, the Blade Witch. This ranged attacker flings a bladed boomerang that can hit you on the way out and then hit you a second time as it returns to the Witch. The Witch can also generate a magic shield that protects her from your attacks between her blade tosses. Watch out for another Corn Hornet shooting at you from the next level up, as well.

After you beat the Drow and Witch, use the bounce pad to hop up and nail the hornet plus two more Spearmen. When you clear the area, a drawbridge **(2)** drops to the next area. Before you cross it, use the teleport pad on the left to find some treasure on another stump then teleport back.

Move forward to meet another spell-casting foe, the Life Spell Punk whose magic heals other enemies nearby. This Punk has an escort of two Drow Spearmen, and he keeps buffing them with an extra +30 hit points every few seconds. Try to target the Punk first. After you KO them all, bounce up to nab the legendary treasure, the Sterling Tapir. Then use the teleport pad to get back down.

Continue to the next platform at the bottom of The Sluice Gate, a long water runoff channel (3). Unfortunately, instead of running water, the sluice channel is running with explosive barrels!

"THE SLUICE GATE" (LIFE)

Grab the Treasure Chest to the right and return to the winch at the bottom of the sluice channel. You must turn the winch to open the gate at the top. Then you must dodge or blast through the rolling barrels to the top before the onscreen timer runs out.

At the top you find a Story Scroll ("History of Flight") to the left, a Treasure Chest to the right, a teleport pad (4) in the center and enemies all over the place, including a Blade Witch and some Drow Spearmen. Clean up the area and use the teleport to zap up to an arena called The Hollow, also strong in the Life element.

"THE HOLLOW" (LIFE)

CLEAR THE HOLLOW

This carved arena is the playground of the dreaded Blitzer Bully. His glowing, charged-up dash attack is similar to the Goliath Drow you met back at the Sky Schooner Docks (Chapter 3), but the Bully features an additional "power" that makes him even tougher to beat: he carries a

Life Spell Punk in his backpack! The Punk bestows fresh hit points (+30 at a shot) on the Bully to keep him healthy.

When you see the Blitzer Bully "charge up" (i.e., start glowing), dodge to the side to avoid his ramming dash then slip around behind and attack to knock the Punk off his back.

Once the Punk is eliminated, you can defeat the Bully much easier.

Use the winch to raise the next gate (5) and hurry on through to grab a big load of treasure and a lift to the next teleport pad. Use the pad to zap back down to The Canopy.

ELEMENTAL GATE: MAGIC

Five Drow Spearmen supported by a Life Spell Punk are posted on the next platform. Clear them off then use a Magic Skylander to unlock the Magic elemental gate (6) on the far side. Cross the bridge to the Ancient Trunk zone, strong in the Magic element, and grab the Soul Gem that unlocks the "Anchor Cannon" power for Gill Grunt.

"ANCIENT TRUNK" (MAGIC)

Now use the nearby teleport pad to reach a small balcony. Use the teleport pad there to arrive at the bottom of a huge, hollowed-out tree trunk (7) lined with platforms connected by a series of bounce pads. The only exit is another teleport pad at the very top. Bounce upward from pad to pad, whacking foes, nabbing the hatbox (and shaking out the Moose Hat), and finally reaching the exit pad.

GET PAST THE CRYSTALS

Drop down to another platform **(8)** guarded by Blade Witches. Use the bounce pads to move around the trunk to a big stickball **(9)**. Push the ball down the winding wooden walkway to wipe out the squad of Drow Spearmen. Follow the ball downhill to the winch. Use the winch to move the swinging platform **(10)** to your side of the gap, but time it so you can run behind the rows of impaling spears as they retract.

At the next platform, run through the impaling spears to the winch **(11)** that opens the next gate. Use the small side planks to avoid the spears when necessary. Once you get through the gate, fight your way through foes to the Treasure Chest at the far right of the connecting walkways. Then battle your way to the energy beam puzzle **(12)**.

A good number of crystals sit on the next stump, but the puzzle is simpler than it looks. Only one crystal is pushable, so push it into the pink beam to redirect energy into the center crystal. Use the lever to rotate the center crystal twice to open the gate.

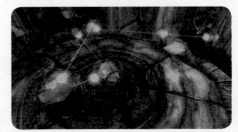

NEW AREA FOUND
"THE SEED TREE" (LIFE)

COLLECT THE LIFE SEEDS

Proceed through the open gate into the final area **(13)**, The Seed Tree, strong in the Life element. It's also crawling with guards, including a pair of Blitzer Bullies. Defeat them all (a difficult fight) to open the gate at the top of the ramp. Then climb up to the Life Seeds and grab them to end the mission.

BACK AT THE RUINS: GRAB THE APPLES!

Arbo plants the Life Seeds to produce apple bushes. But the sheep keep eating the apples! Grab 15 apples before the sheep get them. The sheep seem to know where the next apple is growing even before it appears, so when you see sheep run toward a tree try to beat them there. Once you complete this task, Arbo discovers where the Eternal Life Source is hidden. He also senses that the forest is in danger!

UNCOVER THE WINGED SAPPHIRE

Shoot the rock near Hugo. When it flips over, a Winged Sapphire appears.

11

FALLING FOREST

Talk to Arbo and agree to climb the vine with him to the Falling Forest. This triggers a quick scene: Kaos calls for his Lumberjack Trolls to cut down the Great Ancients of the forest in search of an "acorn"—the Eternal Life Source!

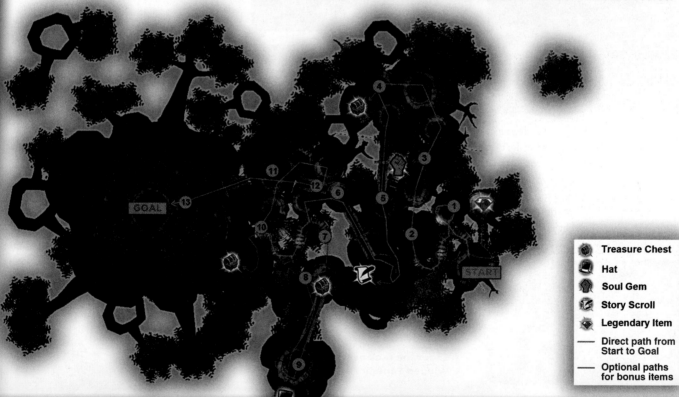

	Treasure Chest
	Hat
	Soul Gem
	Story Scroll
	Legendary Item
—	Direct path from Start to Goal
—	Optional paths for bonus items

OBJECTIVE
FIND THE ETERNAL LIFE SOURCE

ELEMENTAL GATES
EARTH

AREAS TO FIND
OWL'S ROOST
PINECONE'S LANDING
THE ACORN STASH
THE GREAT STUMP

NEW ENEMIES

DARK LIFE
MINION

DARK MISSILE
MINION

DARK NINJA
MINION

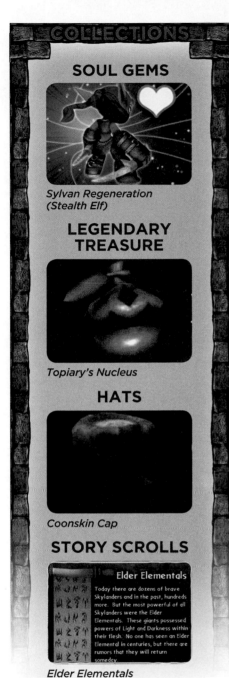

COLLECTIONS

SOUL GEMS

Sylvan Regeneration
(Stealth Elf)

LEGENDARY TREASURE

Topiary's Nucleus

HATS

Coonskin Cap

STORY SCROLLS

Elder Elementals

Today there are dozens of brave Skylanders and in the past, hundreds more. But the most powerful of all Skylanders were the Elder Elementals. These giants possessed powers of Light and Darkness within their flesh. No one has seen an Elder Elemental in centuries, but there are rumors that they will return someday.

Elder Elementals

MISSION GUIDE

Hop down into the Tech-element area of Owl's Roost. Start by veering to the right, where you can step through a gap and drop down to nab a legendary item, the Topiary's Nucleus. Use the bounce pad to get back up and proceed down the curving wooden walkway to the first stump on the right **(1)**.

NEW AREA FOUND
"OWL'S ROOST" (TECH)

DISABLE THE FIRST CHAINSAW

Fight through Troll Greasemonkeys to reach the pile of rockets guarded by a Troll Grenadier. Grab some rockets and continue down the curving walkway, blasting through the wooden gate at the end to reach the troll-operated chainsaw **(2)**. Use the control shown onscreen to fling rockets at the saw until it is disabled. (Six should do the trick.)

Climb the left tread of the disabled vehicle, using the saw-blade as a bridge to the next platform. Wipe out the numerous Troll foes. The path ahead becomes a series of connected platforms with deadly rotating blades. Use the only bounce pad on the first platform **(3)** to reach the Soul Gem ("Sylvan Regeneration" power for Stealth Elf). Use the backmost bounce pad on the fourth platform **(4)** to reach a Treasure Chest.

DISABLE THE SECOND CHAINSAW

Fight your way down the long chute and clear out the next platform **(5)**. Continue across the bridge to the grassy knoll where you find many hostile trolls, a Tech Spell Punk, a Story Scroll (entitled "Elder Elementals"), and most importantly, more rockets!

You must wipe out all foes on the knoll including the Punk in order to open the next gate that leads down to the second chainsaw **(6)**. Blast your way up to grab some rockets and terminate the Punk. Then blast your way down the heavily guarded chute to the chainsaw in a new zone, Pinecone's Landing.

NEW AREA FOUND
"PINECONE'S LANDING" (LIFE)

Once you clear the area, fling rockets at the chainsaw until it breaks. Then climb up the disabled saw, blast the annoying Tech Spell Punk, and continue on left to elemental gate **(7)**.

ELEMENTAL GATE: EARTH

Use an Earth Skylander to unlock the gate and enter the new area, called The Acorn Stash (strong in the Earth element, naturally). Two Troll Grenadiers toss their grenades down from a raised balcony with a Treasure Chest. Unfortunately, you can't reach them from the ground.

NEW AREA FOUND
"THE ACORN STASH" (EARTH)

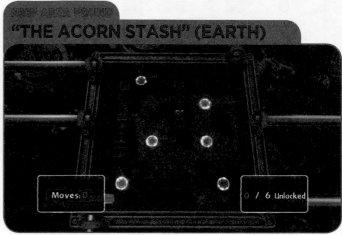

Head straight to the nearby Lock Puzzle **(8)** and select it to bring up the Lock Puzzle interface. To unlock it, turn the Lock Puzzle in the following order: R, L, 2R, 2L, R, L, R, L, 2R, 4L, 3R, L.

When the lock opens, step onto the teleport pad in the alcove beyond to zap to another teleport pad directly above. First, walk from the pad directly off the end of the short ramp to drop onto the Treasure Chest balcony below. Nail the two Grenadiers and shake open the chest.

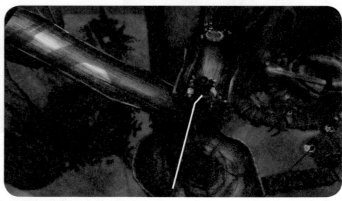

Go to the teleport pad in the alcove again. This time, drop down onto the longer ramp to the left. Follow it to the wooden gate and smash through it. Continue up the ramp and drop down into the arena **(9)** below.

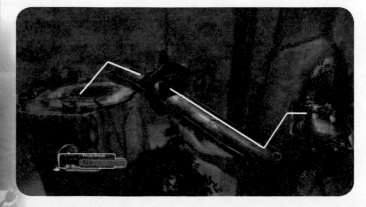

Here's another tough fight! Fend off the Trolls—you must drop them all before the spear gate opens across the arena. When it does, enter and shake open the hatbox to acquire the Coonskin Cap. Use the bounce pad to hop out of the arena back to the long ramp above. Follow that ramp to the end and drop. Now you can exit the Acorn Stash area via the elemental gate.

DISABLE THE THIRD CHAINSAW

Back in the Pinecone's Landing area, fight your way down the curving walkway and smash through the gate. Use the first bounce pad **(10)** to hop up to another Treasure Chest. Use the same pad to bounce across toward the Troll-operated chainsaw **(11)**.

Chances are good here you're either low on rockets or out completely. If so, move past the chainsaw and use a pair of bounce pads to reach another rocket stash **(12)** on a high platform overlooking the big cutting machine. Then drop down and sling six rockets into the chainsaw to disable it.

This fellow spawns a patch of polka-dot mushrooms as a protective barrier, then fires shoulder-mounted missiles from behind this mushroom barrier. Dodge the slow-moving missiles and run around the mushroom thickets to launch attacks. You can also blast right through the mushrooms, but they're sturdy so it takes a few shots.

After you defeat the first Dark Missile Minion, Kaos reappears and summons his Unbeatable Deadly Life Spell of Death, which sends streams of particles that track your Skylander. These inflict damage if they connect, so avoid them. Note that the red particles are destructible—if you shoot a red one, it explodes and detonates all the green particles in its strand too. Use a Skylander with a ranged attack to shoot the red particles!

NEW AREA FOUND
"THE GREAT STUMP"

DEFEAT THE MINIONS OF KAOS

Climb up the chainsaw vehicle to the gate and smash through it to enter the final zone, The Great Stump. Drop down into the arena to trigger the appearance of Kaos. Once again he marshals his minions to attack your Skylander. The first is the Dark Missile Minion.

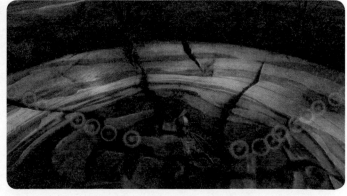

Next, Kaos sends in his second lackey, the Dark Ninja Minion. This fighter is a dark version of the Stealth Elf Skylander, wielding twin knives and a lightning dash attack.

After you take out the Dark Ninja Minion, Kaos summons more long strands of particles. (He calls this one his "Totally Unbeatable Deadly Evil Life Spell of Ultimate Death.") Again, shoot at the red particles to destroy the entire string. Some all-green strands try to enclose your Skylander in circles or spirals, but there's always a gap that you can hustle through to avoid getting caught and taking damage.

If you caome out alive, Kaos sends in his final lackey, a twisted tree stump monster. This lackey hacks out two different types of seed, both of which simply roll dangerously around the arena if they miss. The larger seed is explosive and inflicts heavy damage if it strikes; the smaller seeds spit out in pairs and wrap their target in movement-slowing vines if they hit. (You can escape the vines by jiggling the control shown onscreen.)

After you defeat the Dark Life Minion, more particle strings twirl into the arena. Run in circles while firing to avoid the green strands and destroy the red ones. Finally, you face the ultimate test: all three minions plus the ongoing particle strands. Keep up your circling and firing. Try to target just one minion at a time until he falls—you want to minimize the amount of time you have to face all three at once.

Good luck! When the last of the three minions falls, Kaos finally gives up and lets you have the Eternal Life Source.

BACK AT THE RUINS

Watch as the Eternal Life Source takes its place in the Core of Light. As Hugo says, four down, four to go! General Robot reports that the trolls have the Golden Gear stashed in a heavily guarded warehouse. Hugo explains that you need that gear to rebuild the Core of Light!

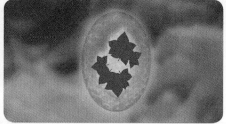

12
TROLL WAREHOUSE

Talk to General Robot and agree to travel to the Troll Warehouse. Your Skylander travels by cannon to the gates at Research Base Omega. There you meet Snuckles, the same fellow you met in the very first mission on Shattered Island. He's joined the Mabu Defense Force as a special agent, and he leads you into the warehouse access elevator.

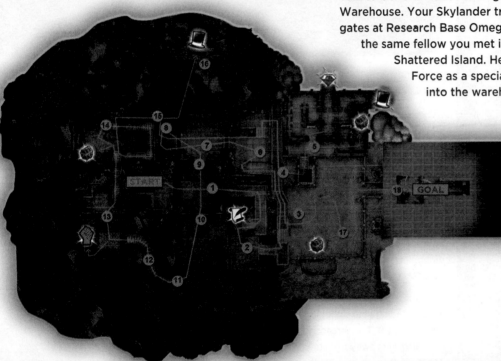

	Treasure Chest
	Hat
	Soul Gem
	Story Scroll
	Legendary Item
——	Direct path from Start to Goal
——	Optional paths for bonus items

OBJECTIVES
FIND THE TROLL WAREHOUSE
FIND THE PIECES OF THE MAP
GET THROUGH THE MINEFIELD

ELEMENTAL GATES
FIRE
LIFE

AREAS TO FIND
RESEARCH BASE OMEGA
ISOLATION CELLS
THE FOUNDRY
THE MINEFIELD
ACCESS CATWALKS
LAVA REFUGE
WAREHOUSE

NEW ENEMIES

TROLLVERINE

ROCKET IMP

GUN SNOUT

LAVA KING

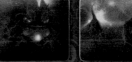
FLAME IMPS

MISSION GUIDE

This starting base is strong in the Life element, so consider switching to a Life Skylander. The entry door is locked with a Lock Puzzle. Bring up the Lock Puzzle interface and turn the box in the following sequence: 5L, 6R, L.

COLLECTIONS

SOUL GEMS

MIRV Mortar
(Zook)

LEGENDARY TREASURE

Ghost View Glasses

HATS

Spy Gear

Rocket Hat

STORY SCROLLS

The game of BOOM!

The game of BOOM!

NEW AREA FOUND
"RESEARCH BASE OMEGA" (LIFE)

NEW AREA FOUND
"THE FOUNDRY"

Once the area is cleared, you face another Lock Puzzle. Turn the box in the following sequence: L, R, L, 2R, 4L. For the Wii, the solution is 2R, L, R, 2L.

When the door opens, go through to meet another new foe, the Rocket Imp. This little monster gets a real kick out of his destructive habits. True to his name, he fires mini-rockets from his pistol-like handheld launcher. The projectiles travel just slow enough to dodge, but as you get closer the rockets have less distance to travel and thus become more difficult to avoid. Pay attention to the Imp's firing pattern: he shoots three times in a row then pauses to reload. Rush him immediately after his third shot!

The Rocket Imp runs away if you attack then let up, leading your right into an ambush of other foes **(2)**. Try retreating to pull one or two attackers away from the group, finish them off, then go back for the others. When the battle is over you can grab the Story Scroll entitled "The Game of Boom!"

Continue on until you reach an empty-looking dirt lot **(3)** that triggers a cinematic: Snuckles spots the Golden Gear in the warehouse across the lot. Unfortunately, the lot is a deadly minefield! Snuckles surmises that a minefield map must exist somewhere and suggests you go find it. There's no crossing the minefield without one.

FIND THE WAREHOUSE

Enter The Foundry and face a vicious new foe, the Trollverine **(1)**. This goon wields three razor-sharp claws on one arm and uses the other to hold up an impenetrable shield as he charges at you. Fortunately, the Trollverine's attack is so frenzied that when he swings, he loses his balance a bit and teeters backward. Counterstrike when he's off-balance in order to inflict damage!

NEW AREA FOUND
"THE MINEFIELD"

ELEMENTAL GATE: LIFE

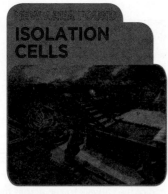

Snuckles stays behind. Just ahead is a Life elemental gate. Use a Life Skylander to unlock it and cross the magic vine bridge. Enter the security complex **(5)** filled with keys and locked rooms.

In three separate locked rooms you can find a Treasure Chest, a hatbox with the Spy Gear, and a legendary item called the Ghost View Glasses. Unfortunately there are only enough keys to unlock two of these three items. The walkthrough leads to the hat and the legendary item, leaving the chest for a subsequent visit.

Using the numbers on the overhead screenshot, do the following:

- Grab the key at 1 and unlock the door at 2.
- Grab the keys at 3 and 4 and unlock the door at 5.
- Grab the key at 6 and unlock the door at 7.
- Grab both keys at 8 and unlock the door at 9.
- Solve the Lock Puzzle at 10 by turning the lockbox in the following sequence: 3L, R, L, R, 2L, R, 3L.
- Grab both keys at 11 and 12.
- Unlock the door at 13 and grab the Ghost View Glasses at 14.
- Unlock the doors at 15, 16, and 17.
- Grab the hatbox with the Spy Gear hat at 18.

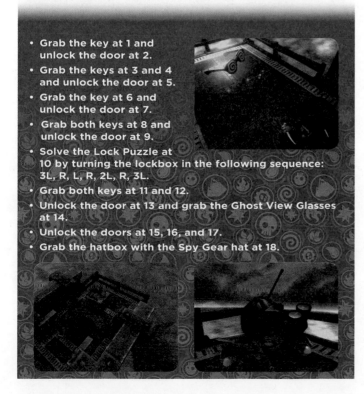

Exit the security complex and go back through the Life elemental gate to exit the area.

FIND THE FOUR MAP PIECES

Now you must assemble the minefield map that is scattered around the complex in four pieces. Go down the ramp to find the first map piece **(6)** floating in the room.

When you clear the room of enemies (including another dangerous Trollverine) the security door to the left slides open. Proceed into the next room **(7)** to face a towering new menace, the Gun Snout—a walker vehicle piloted by a Troll Greasemonkey.

Several Troll infantry are posted here too—you might want to eliminate them first, luring them out of the Gun Snout's range. The Gun Snout hops before it fires 12 powerful rounds, then pauses and repeats the sequence. Attack after the shooting stops, but get some distance when you see that walker hop! When the machine finally falls, don't ease up—the Troll driver hops out and attacks.

When the room is clear, go to the next security door Lock Puzzle and solve the Lock Puzzle by turning the box in the following sequence: R, 5L, 2R, 3L, 2R. The solution for the Wii is: 5R, 3L.

When the door opens, enter the next room and grab the second map piece **(8)** then push the red button to open two more security gates. Go through both newly opened gates at **(9)** and **(10)** into a room with a crystal puzzle.

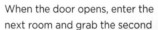

REDIRECT THE ENERGY BEAM

Your goal here is to redirect the energy beam to the crystal lock on the gear-shaped door **(11)** in the back right corner of the room. Go toward the far wall and push the movable box to the left. (The beam should hit it now.) Push the movable crystal next to that box twice so it points at the door crystal.

Now push the moveable box on the right side of the room forward once. Push the movable crystal next to it three times so it slides into the energy beam.

Finally, use the floor lever to turn the rotating crystal once. This routes the energy beam to the gear-shaped door and opens it.

Here's what the finished arrangement looks like:

Exit via the newly opened door and look for the third map piece **(12)** on the curving walkway beyond. Continue into the next room where another Troll squad led by a Gun Snout waits to inflict pain. Take them out and grab the Soul Gem that unlocks the "MIRV Mortar" power for Zook.

Another Lock Puzzle **(13)** blocks your way. Here's the solution sequence: 5R, 3L. The Wii solution is: R, L, R, L, R, 3L, R, L, R. When the door opens, proceed into a new zone, the Access Catwalks, strong in the Tech element.

NEW AREA FOUND
"ACCESS CATWALKS" (TECH)

CLEAR THE CATWALKS

Follow the catwalk to the drop-off point and, well, drop off. This is a heavily defended room full of the usual Troll suspects, including another lumbering Gun Snout. Clear the area and grab the Treasure Chest,

then smash through the wooden gate **(14)** and climb the stairs on the far side. These lead to the final puzzle piece **(15)** on the catwalks. Just beyond is an elemental gate.

ELEMENTAL GATE: FIRE

Switch to a Fire Skylander, unlock the gate, and step into the fiery exhaust pipe just beyond. This shoots you down to the Lava Refuge zone below **(16)**, where Fire Skylanders have a definite advantage! (They can walk on lava.) Walk across the lava to the left to face new foes, a pair of big Lava Kings who can spew out Flame Imps, described as "droplets of possessed magma." Extinguish the threat!

NEW AREA FOUND
"LAVA REFUGE" (FIRE)

After you clear the area, solve the nearby Lock Puzzle by turning the lockbox in the following sequence: L, 8R, L, 3R, L, 2R, L, R, 4L, 2R. Then shake open the hatbox inside to get the Rocket Hat, which adds a whopping +6 to your Speed! Return to the teleport pad to zap back up to the Access Catwalks.

CROSS THE MINEFIELD

Now that you have all four puzzle pieces, use the teleport pad at the end of the catwalk to zap across the complex. Follow the next catwalk down and return to the edge of the minefield **(3)** where Snuckles waits. He congratulates you on finding the map, and the safe path now appears as a dotted line superimposed on the minefield. Follow the route carefully!

When you reach the spot **(17)** circled on the overhead shot, you can veer safely to the Treasure Chest. Return to the dotted line and follow it all the way to the red X in the Warehouse area. This triggers the final scene as you complete the mission.

NEW AREA FOUND
"WAREHOUSE"

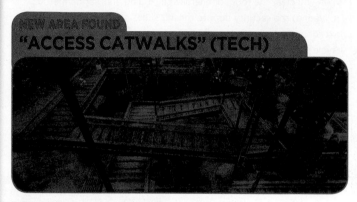

BACK AT THE RUINS

Watch as the Golden Gear is inserted into the Core of Light. Unfortunately, you need some Green Primordial Goo to lubricate the works. This means a strike into the heart of Troll country!

13

GOO FACTORY

Talk to General Robot and agree to travel to the Goo Factory. Cannon-propelled flight lands your chosen Skylander in the rainy trenches just outside the factory. Snuckles meets you again and reports a missing squad of soldiers. Your first task is to find them and talk to their Mabu captain!

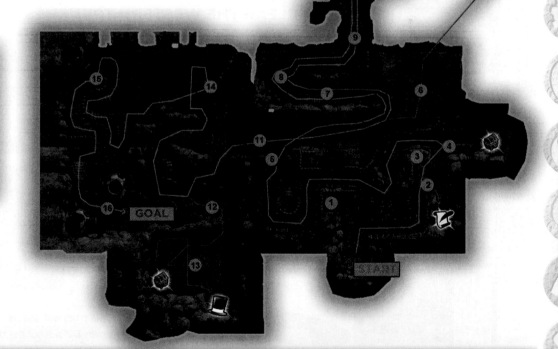

- Treasure Chest
- Hat
- Soul Gem
- Story Scroll
- Legendary Item
- —— Direct path from Start to Goal
- —— Optional paths for bonus items

OBJECTIVES
FIND THE MABU CAPTAIN
LEVEL THE WALL WITH A MEGA BOMB
RAISE ALL GOO FACTORY FLAGS

ELEMENTAL GATE
AIR
FIRE

AREAS TO FIND
WESTERN TRENCHES
SANDBAG HILL
POTATO FARM
THE AMMO DUMP
TWENTY STONE DEFENSE

NEW ENEMIES
NONE

COLLECTIONS

SOUL GEMS

Orbiting Sun Shield
(Camo)

LEGENDARY TREASURE

Troll Stein

HATS

General's Hat

Spiked Hat

STORY SCROLLS

Evolution of Trolls

Trolls once lived under bridges and made anyone who crossed over pay them a toll. But in truth, most people got over the bridge without paying a toll, using billy-goats, "Fools Gold" and "Fools Potatoes". So the trolls gave up collecting tolls, crawled out from under their bridges and went to work for Kaos.

Evolution of Trolls

MISSION GUIDE

You start in the Western Trenches, strong naturally in the Earth element. Here's a quick tip to make things a bit easier: Veer leftward into the first area to find a reusable bomb **(1)**. Toss a few bombs down into the trenches just beyond to take out a few enemies. Now you won't need to fight them later.

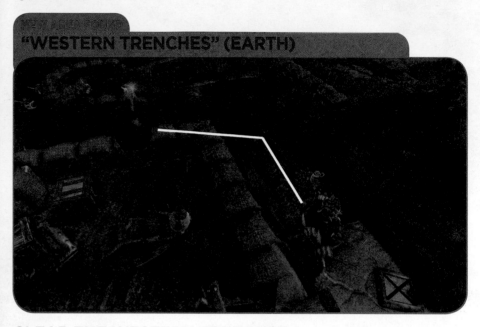

NEW AREA FOUND

"WESTERN TRENCHES" (EARTH)

CLEAR THE WESTERN TRENCHES

Proceed down the trench to the right. Blast through the debris blocking the trench and then climb up the hill on the right **(2)** to nail the Troll Grenadier and nab the Story Scroll (entitled "Evolution of Trolls.")

Continue along the trench, veer left up to another reusable bomb **(3)**, and toss a few bombs down on the Trolls in the trench below. Bring a bomb down into the trench to the purple bomb icon **(4)** on the right. Toss the bomb at the barricade there to blast your way to the Treasure Chest.

Continue up the winding trench—the way should be largely clear of Trolls if you did your bomb-tossing earlier as suggested! Keep going until you meet Rizzo, the Mabu Captain **(5)**. He reports that the main factories are just up ahead, but a big wall stands in the way and some Troll turrets have your forces pinned down. But a scout has discovered a stockpile of Mega-Bombs in the ammo dump at the top of the hill to the right. Just one of those can bust the wall and KO the turrets!

Head up the trench to the right to a new area, Sandbag Hill. Watch out! Troll artillery has spotted you and its yellow aiming reticle starts tracking your Skylander. When the reticle reaches a target it turns into a red crosshairs and the shell drops on that spot soon after. Keep moving until you reach the elemental gate ahead on the right!

NEW AREA FOUND
"SANDBAG HILL" (EARTH)

ELEMENTAL GATE: AIR

Switch to an Air Skylander to unlock the gate then step through into the whirlwind. It transports your Skylander to a high plateau called Potato Farm, strong in the Air element. The field is full of land mines, but you can use the bounce pads to hop over each line of mines. Keep hopping until you reach the hut in the field's back left corner—the doors automatically open, revealing a teleport pad. Use that pad to zap into a structure with a hatbox containing the General's Hat. Return to the field via the nearby teleport.

NEW AREA FOUND
"POTATO FARM" (AIR)

Use the bounce pad in the back right corner of the field to hop up onto the wooden platform and drop into the ravine beyond. There you find a Rocket Imp and an Earth Spell

Punk guarding a legendary treasure called the Troll Stein. Terminate the Imp and Punk, grab the treasure, and use the teleport pad to zap back across the field. Use the whirlwind to return to the trenches below.

DESTROY THE DEFENSE WALLS!

Note the reusable bomb near the lava pit. Head left and clear out the Trolls guarding the barricade **(7)**. Then double back, grab a bomb, and go toss it at the barricade to clear the trench.

Another reusable bomb **(8)** is nearly hidden in the debris where the trench curls back to the right. Blast a path through the debris and then haul a bomb up to destroy

the next barricade **(9)** where the three Troll cannons are firing their barrage.

Now proceed up the path into The Ammo Dump zone (strong in the Tech element) and talk to Nort. Nort leads up an alternate path—a back-door route into the Troll ammo dump!

NEW AREA FOUND
"THE AMMO DUMP" (TECH)

Follow him up to a ledge overlooking the open yard behind the Troll breastworks. Drop down and wipe out the Troll troops in the yard, including a Mark 31 Troll Tank. Enter the next yard and find the Soul Gem in the back right corner. (It unlocks the "Orbiting Sun Shield" power for Camo.) Next, clear the way to the Mega Bomb pen **(10)** in the back left corner of the ammo dump. Don't miss the Treasure Chest (circled in the shot) just behind the pen!

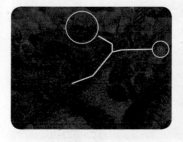

Smash open the pen's gate and walk your Skylander directly into the first Mega Bomb to push it. Use your character to keep nudging the bomb downhill until it rolls into the breastworks and destroys the wall.

Go retrieve another Mega Bomb and start rolling it downhill. Push it all the way down the trench until it rolls into the main defense wall **(11)** and demolishes it. Watch out for the two Troll Turrets. They try to push your Skylander off course.

Rizzo points out the three Troll factories. He wants you to capture each one and raise its flag to signal the Mabu troops. Before you assault the factories, however, go to the elemental gate **(12)** just off the main trench to the left.

ELEMENTAL GATE: FIRE

Use a Fire Skylander to unlock the gate. Walk across the lava pond beyond it and enter the zone called Twenty Stone Defense **(13)**. Your goal here is to push blocks around so that you can reach both the Treasure Chest and the hatbox with the Spiked Hat inside.

NEW AREA FOUND
"TWENTY STONE DEFENSE" (FIRE)

- **Push the blocks at 1 and 2 to the right.**
- **Push the block at 3 back against the wall.**
- **Push the block at 4 twice to the right.**
- **Push the blocks at 5 and 6 to the left.**
- **Push the block at 7 over once.**
- **Step on the teleport pad at 8 to reach 9 and shake open the Treasure Chest.**
- **Push the block at 10 back to where it started (at 4) and then go climb the ramp.**
- **Push the block at 11 once so it falls into the gap.**
- **Now walk across the tops of the blocks over to the hatbox on the raised platform.**

Just for reference, here's what it should look like when finished:

Exit the Twenty Stone Defense area and turn left to launch your assault up Sandbag Hill.

RAISE THE THREE FACTORY FLAGS

Fight up the trench to the first factory **(14)**. Clear the area and approach the flagpole. Rotate the control as shown onscreen to raise the flag. One down, two to go!

Advance toward the second factory **(15)**. Projectiles come fast and furious here—a Rocket Imp, several Troll Grenadiers, and a Mark 31 Troll Tank make the going tough. Fight through them to the second flagpole and raise the flag.

Now make your final assault. Hammer your way across to the third factory flagpole **(16)**, wiping out all resistance. Raise the flag to complete the mission. The Mabu forces collect the required goo and return to the Ruins.

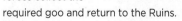

BACK AT THE RUINS

Watch as the Green Goo of Primordia greases the gears of the Core of Light. Afterwards, General Robot reports that the Trolls have the Eternal Tech Source hidden in their base.

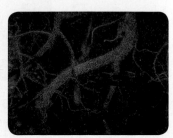

14

BATTLEFIELD

Talk to General Robot and agree to travel to the Battlefield. Upon your arrival, Snuckles gives you a situation report: not good. The Trolls are winning! They've overrun your defenses and the Mabu Command Team is cut off from the rest of the force.

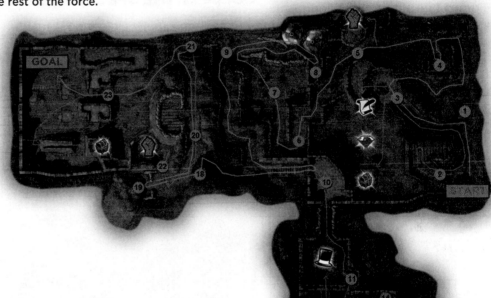

	Treasure Chest
	Hat
	Soul Gem
	Story Scroll
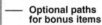	Legendary Item
——	Direct path from Start to Goal
——	Optional paths for bonus items

OBJECTIVES
FIND THE COMMAND TEAM

GET THE ETERNAL TECH SOURCE FROM THE FORT

ELEMENTAL GATES
UNDEAD

AREAS TO FIND
SOUTHERN TRENCHES

THE BIRD'S NEST

DEFENSIVE PERIMETER

NO MAN'S LAND

THE STADIUM

TECH BASE THETA

NEW ENEMIES

BOSS TROLL
SUPER TANK

COLLECTIONS

SOUL GEMS

Arkeyan Armor
(Drill Sergeant)

Afterburners
(Drobot)

LEGENDARY TREASURE

Royal Lynx

HATS

Combat Hat

STORY SCROLLS

Special Order 31

A note from a troll commander says "Strange and odd behavior attracts fire from enemy positions, which might result in injury, so please refrain from the following activities: barbwire tug-o-war, minefield races, and hand grenade juggling contests."

Special Order 31

MISSION GUIDE

You start in the Southern Trenches, strong in the Tech element. First off, collect a few special items. See the barricade (2) with a purple bomb icon just up the stairs to the left? Veer up the trench to the right to find a bomb (1) then run it back and toss it at the barricade.

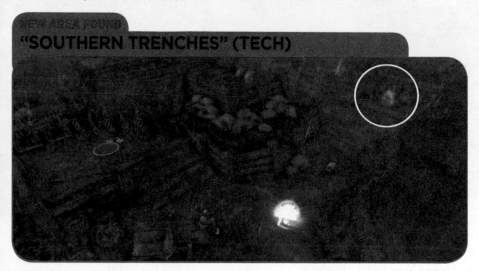

NEW AREA FOUND

"SOUTHERN TRENCHES" (TECH)

COLLECT THE SPECIAL ITEMS

Climb to a new zone called The Bird's Nest. Fire the cannon to blast the structure in the open field; this reveals a legendary treasure, the Royal Lynx. A Treasure Chest also sits on the far edge of the field.

NEW AREA FOUND

"THE BIRD'S NEST"

Go back down to the Southern Trenches, grab another bomb, and run it up to the next barricade (3). After you blast it open, engage the big Gun Snout and other Troll troops just beyond. Clear the area and climb up onto the stone rampart to grab the Story Scroll entitled "Special Order 31."

Go down into the field—a new zone called the Defensive Perimeter, strong in the Fire element. Careful! Land mines make it a deadly space. Work carefully around the mine clusters to retrieve the Royal Lynx (the legendary treasure you revealed earlier with the cannon shot) as well as the Treasure Chest and other loot. Then return to the Southern Trenches.

NEW AREA FOUND
"DEFENSIVE PERIMETER" (FIRE)

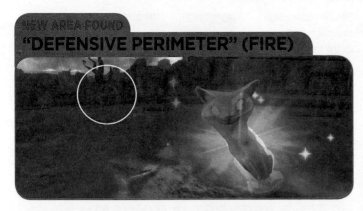

CROSS THE DEFENSIVE PERIMETER

Work your way down the trench to find the key **(4)** on the platform guarded by a pair of dangerous Trollverines and a Blaster Troll. Patiently defeat these foes: remember, each hit from a Trollverine inflicts heavy damage, so get away when they wind up to strike! Grab the key and use it to unlock the gate up ahead **(5)** but don't miss the destructible wall on the right, just before the gate. Smash through it to find a Soul Gem that unlocks "Arkeyan Armor" power for the Tech Skylander named Drill Sergeant.

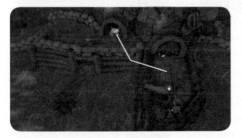

Fight your way along the trench and wipe out all foes to open the spear gate **(6)**. Proceed into a big, arena-like yard **(7)** where you must eliminate a Gun Snout, then take out the two Troll Greasemonkeys that appear, in order to open the next spear gate on the yard's far side. Beyond that, a defensive wall **(9)** blocks your way, so climb the hill to the right and use the teleport pad in the house to zap over to the cannon **(8)** on the nearby rampart. Take out the guard then use the cannon to blast open the defensive wall across the yard. Teleport back and go through the breach.

Fight down the trench until it splits. Go left first to a staircase that leads up onto a platform **(10)** with another cannon and an elemental gate. Fire the cannon to destroy a guard tower **(18)** further up the trench; this reveals a key in the tower. (Another Gun Snout is posted right next to it.) Then approach the elemental gate.

ELEMENTAL GATE: UNDEAD

Switch to an Undead Skylander to unlock the gate and cross the bone bridge into No Man's Land. You see a hatbox atop a staircase but a wall blocks access—note the Mega Bomb icon on the ground by the wall. Step on the teleport pad **(11)** in the back left corner to zap down to a dark basement.

NEW AREA FOUND
"NO MAN'S LAND" (UNDEAD)

Use the bounce pad to hop over the raised walkway and smash through the breakable wall to reach the Mega Bombs **(12)**. Push a big bomb down the ramp then over to the left onto another Mega Bomb icon to blast open the barricade. Step onto the floor button **(13)** (circled in the screenshot) to lower the two nearby blocks.

Now push another Mega Bomb over the two lowered blocks and into the alcove formed by four lowered blocks **(14)**. Use the bounce pad on the right to hop up to the raised walkway. Follow the walkway to another floor button and step on it to raise the four-block section, lifting the bomb up to the walkway level.

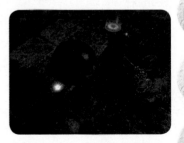

The next objective is a Treasure Chest. Push the big bomb along the raised walkway to the Mega Bomb icon at the end **(15)** and blow up the wall to get the Treasure Chest behind it.

Go back along the raised walkway and step on the floor button to lower the four blocks you just raised. Now go get another Mega Bomb and repeat the previous process to get it up onto the raised walkway. But this time push it down the short ramp to another floor button **(16)** at the bottom of a narrow ramp leading up.

When the Mega Bomb sits on this button, the nearby spear gate lowers. Step on the floor button behind the gate **(17)** to raise a three-block section at the top of the ramp. Push the bomb up the ramp and across these three newly raised blocks until it drops in the next room and blows up the barricade leading up to the hatbox. Shake open the box to get the Combat Hat, then exit No Man's Land.

FIND THE COMMAND TEAM

Fire the cannon if you haven't already done so (you have if you have followed this walkthrough up to this point) and fight your way up the trench past the Gun Snout. Grab the key in the tower **(18)** and note the double-locked gate nearby. Continue left to grab a second key **(19)** and note the Mega Bomb icon at a barricade that blocks access to a Soul Gem. Now use both keys on the double-locked gate **(20)**.

Go through the gate and find the Command Team in the sandbag enclosure just up the hill. Captain Rizzo explains the tactical situation and sends you on to the Mega Bomb stockpile **(21)** just up the trench.

DEFEAT THE SUPER TANK

Push the first Mega Bomb all the way back to the bomb icon **(22)**. Bomb the barricade and collect the Soul Gem that unlocks the "Afterburners" power for Drobot. Then return to the stockpile and push another Mega Bomb out into the open field called The Stadium, strong in the Undead element. Guide the bomb right into the nearest wall **(23)** to blast it open. This explosion unleashes the Troll secret weapon, a massive tank powered by the Eternal Tech Source!

NEW AREA FOUND
"THE STADIUM" (UNDEAD)

Before you engage the mech-beast, go to the far left side of this final zone (called Tech Base Theta) and use a Troll Bomb to blast the top left corner Troll Turret. Use a Bounce Pad to reach the Treasure Chest up on the rampart.

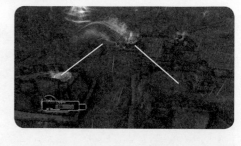

NEW AREA FOUND
"TECH BASE THETA" (UNDEAD)

Now start grabbing the reusable bombs from the two platforms in the base and start tossing them at the Troll Super Tank. When you finally destroy it, the Eternal Tech Source rises. Walk underneath to collect it and complete the mission.

BACK AT THE RUINS: INVESTIGATE THE BEACH

Watch as the Eternal Tech Source takes its place in the Core of Light, and a strange new development shakes things up down on the beach! Head downstairs to the spooky door to meet T-Bone, the talking skull. He asks your Skylander for help in gathering the other bones for his "body."

Follow the dotted line to find the rest of Mr. T-Bone, piece by piece. You must do a little turtle pushing, but you're good at that now. When you find all the skeleton parts, Hugo arrives to talk about what's needed for the next Core of Light component, the Eternal Undead Source.

15 CRAWLING CATACOMBS

Talk to T-Bone at the underworld door down by the beach. Agree to descend the stairs into the Crawling Catacombs. When you arrive, your skeletal guide gets spooked off, leaving your Skylander to operate alone.

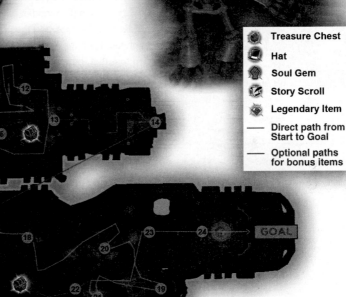

Treasure Chest

Hat

Soul Gem

Story Scroll

Legendary Item

— Direct path from Start to Goal

— Optional paths for bonus items

START

GOAL

OBJECTIVES
FIND THE SKULL MASK

ELEMENTAL GATES
UNDEAD

AREAS TO FIND
PIT OF WEBS
ALCHEMY LAB
CHAMBER OF EYES
THE SKITTERING DARK
THE WIDOW'S COURT

NEW ENEMIES

 SPIDER SWARMER

 SPIDER SPITTER

 FAT BELLY SPIDER

 MOON WIDOW

 GARGANTULA

COLLECTIONS

SOUL GEMS

Spyro's Earth Pound (Spyro)

LEGENDARY TREASURE

Aphid Lifter

HATS

Beret

STORY SCROLLS

Eon's origin

I, Eon, began my life as a humble servant boy, polishing pans in the kitchen of the Portal Master Nattybumpo. People realized I was no normal boy when, at the age of 8, I activated Nattybumpo's own portal and teleported him, possibly accidentally, into the middle of the Dirt Sea.

Eon's origin

MISSION GUIDE

Bash through the wall into the Pit of Webs, an area strong in the Undead element. You immediately encounter a new monster, the tiny but lethal Spider Swarmer. True to their name, these arachnids tend to travel in swarms. They speed-rush your Skylander, then start glowing red and suddenly explode into a deadly green cloud. Blast them before they can get in close!

NEW AREA FOUND
"PIT OF WEBS" (UNDEAD)

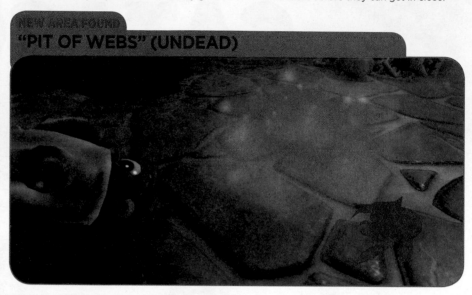

FIND THE THREE KEYS

Smash through the wooden gate on the right **(1)** to enter the Alchemy Lab. Bash all the stuff inside to gather loot, and then collect the Story Scroll entitled "Eon's Origin." Exit the lab and continue down the Pit of Webs passage, blasting Spider Swarmers from afar. Grab the bomb **(2)** and toss it at the wall marked by the bomb icon **(3)** to demolish it.

NEW AREA FOUND
"ALCHEMY LAB" (UNDEAD)

FIRST KEY

Go through the breach to find pod-like Spider Spitters that spit out the little Spider Swarmers you've been swatting so far. Blast the pods to stop the spider-production then continue around the corner to the bounce pads. Use them to hop up to collect the first key on the top platform.

Take the key down the corridor and use it on one of the three locks on the triple-locked gate **(8)**. The camera gives you a quick glimpse of the other two keys, and then you meet your first Fat Belly Spider. This nasty creature tries to get close and then secretes a green pool of Spider Goo that inflicts painful damage. The Fat Belly is invulnerable during this secretion stage, so stay back until it regains its fat-bellied shape. Then defeat it!

SECOND KEY

Check the wall opposite the triple-locked gate and smash the breakable items. Use the Bounce Pad to jump up on the raised platform **(4)** and grab a bomb. Quickly hop back down and toss the bomb at the nearby wall **(5)** marked with a bomb icon to blast it open.

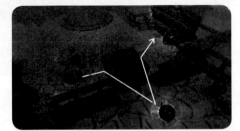

More Fat Belly Spiders attack as you move through the breach, and you see a thievin' little Hob 'n' Yaro swipe the second key **(6)**. You can't catch or hit him with normal attacks as he runs in circles around the crypt, so dispatch the spiders and go grab another bomb **(4)**. Run it back and toss it over the crypt at the Hob 'n' Yaro.

The Hob 'n' Yaro's demise also opens the nearby gate to the Soul Gem that unlocks the "Spyro's Earth Pound" power for Spyro. (Ignore the lovely legendary treasure spinning behind the other spear gate—you can't collect it yet.) Take the second key back and use it on the locked gate **(8)**. Only one lock left!

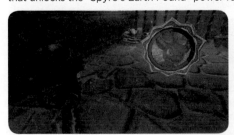

THIRD KEY

Grab another bomb **(4)** and run it down to the icon-marked wall **(7)** by the crypt. Toss the bomb to blast open the wall, kill the Fat Belly Spider on the other side, and grab the third key. Use it to finish unlocking the gate **(8)**.

As you move down the next corridor the "lights" go out—i.e., visibility is restricted to a small circle around your Skylander. Proceed leftward to find the elemental gate **(9)** which also has many Spider Spitters near it.

ELEMENTAL GATE: UNDEAD

Use an Undead Skylander to unlock the gate and enter the Chamber of Eyes **(10)**, a room with five alcoves off the central chamber. Refer to the numbered screenshot. A bomb floats in the middle of the room. Alcoves 1 to 4 have eye switches inside—hence the chamber's name. You must activate all four eye switches to open the gate leading into alcove 5 where a hatbox is stored.

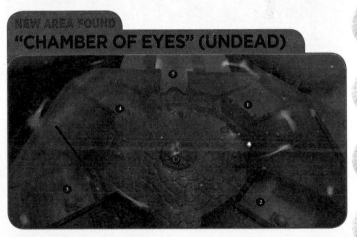

NEW AREA FOUND
"CHAMBER OF EYES" (UNDEAD)

Now take the following steps:

- Grab the bomb at B and toss it at the icon-marked wall at 1 to open the switch alcove. (Take your time—there's no rush yet.)
- Knock down the breakable wall to open alcove 2.
- Check out alcove 3 and note the spinning blade moving back and forth.
- Check out alcove 4 and note the impaling spears thrusting up from the floor.

- Note that hitting each eye switch triggers a timer that gives you 5 seconds to hit the next switch.
- Move to the center of the room where the reusable bomb floats.
- Toss bombs quickly at all four switches to activate them, hitting each switch before the 5-second timer runs out from the previous switch.
- When all four switches are active, the alcove 5 gate drops to the floor. Sprint through the lowered gate and grab the hatbox.
- Shake the Beret (+15 Critical Hit) out of the hatbox and exit the Chamber of Eyes.

TAKE A LEGENDARY DETOUR

As you exit the elemental gate back into the Pit of Webs, visibility narrows again to a small circle around your Skylander. Smash through the breakable wooden gate on the far wall and hack through the bone pile and a Spider Spitter. Move slowly here! Some impaling spears **(11)** are just ahead, at the top of the stairs; you can't see them until you're almost on top of them.

The next corridor features another gate **(12)** controlled by eye switches. But a new foe, the Moon Widow spider, lays its sticky web across your path, slowing you down to make you easier prey for other spiders. Avoid the Widow's web strands and eliminate her. If your Skylander becomes tangled in webs, shake your controller to escape.

A reusable bomb floats in front of the gate. Grab and toss bombs quickly at the two eye switches on either side of the gate to lock it in the open position.

Now you need to blast open another wall up ahead. Grab another bomb from **(12)** and sprint upstairs. Watch out for more impaling spears at the top! Time your run past them and then toss the bomb at the wall **(13)** to gain access to a block puzzle chamber.

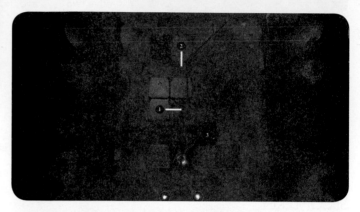

Refer to the screenshot for the following instructions to create a raised route across the room:

- Push the block at 1 to the right.
- Push the block at 2 toward the camera.
- Climb the ramp and smash the barrels on the block at 3.

Yes, it's just that simple because you can run diagonally from block to block, albeit carefully. Now grab a bomb, follow the red route, and then toss the bomb

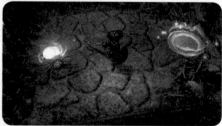

against the back wall **(14)**. This reveals a teleport pad. Use the pad to collect the legendary item you passed earlier, the Aphid Lifter. Teleport back and cross the chamber to the bomb on the ramp.

COLLECT TWO CHESTS

Grab a bomb, exit the chamber, and then follow the corridor to the right to another bomb icon **(15)**. Toss the bomb to demolish the wall and grab the Treasure Chest.

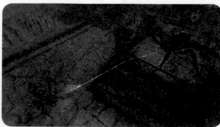

Move carefully past the spinning blades and impaling spears to find a few Moon Widows and a big Gargantula up on a platform **(16)**. The massive spider is sitting on the key you need to open the locked gate behind her. The Gargantula shoots a strand of web at its prey and pulls it in close for feeding.

Dodge the entangling strands and exterminate the Gargantula. Grab the key and open the gate. Just beyond the gate is a destructible wall **(17)** marked by a bomb icon. Go back and grab a bomb to blast it open and shake open another Treasure Chest.

Follow the corridor down the stairs. Your visibility is restricted once again as you enter a new zone called The Skittering Dark, strong in the Fire element.

NEW AREA FOUND

"THE SKITTERING DARK" (FIRE)

FIND TWO KEYS

Smash through the wooden fence and enter the next, foe-filled room **(18)** where a big pile of bones covers a fiery grate. Stick to the right-hand wall and follow it just past a spear-gate with a Treasure Chest on the other side—you can't reach the chest yet. Now stick to the left-hand wall and continue, but be ready for Fat Belly Spiders! Continue along the left wall until you reach the double-locked gate **(23)**. Then check out the overhead screenshots.

Down the slope to the right of the double-locked gate is a destructible wall (circled in the screenshot) marked by a bomb icon and guarded by a Gargantula plus a pair of Moon Widows. The first key **(19)** is behind that wall. Wipe out the spiders, return uphill to the gate, then walk toward the camera to find the alcove with a bomb and multiple Spider Spitters **(20)**. Grab a bomb and run it back down to blast the wall and grab the first key.

From the first key, walk your Skylander toward the camera across the fiery grate and past the spinning blades. Enter the first room on the right to find a Moon Widow, a Spider Spitter and the second key **(21)**. Note the bomb icon **(22)** on the floor nearby—another Treasure Chest sits behind this destructible wall. Take both keys back to the double-locked gate and unlock it. Before you go through the gate, grab another bomb from **(20)** and run it back to get the Treasure Chest behind **(22)**. (It's a long run so you might want to switch to your fastest Skylander before you try it.)

FIND THE SKULL MASK

Go through the gate and drop into the final chamber, called The Widow's Court **(24)**—not a cheery sounding name. (Skylanders of the Magic element are strongest here.) Your full vision finally returns, but you may wish it didn't: spiders of all shapes and sizes drop in for dinner. Just when you think you've nearly cleared the room, more and bigger spiders arrive. Keep circling as you fire and try to avoid the webbing traps. Find the Skull Mask

Go through the gate and drop into the final chamber, called The Widow's Court **(24)**—not a cheery sounding name. (Skylanders of the Magic element are strongest here.) Your full vision finally returns, but you may wish it didn't: spiders of all shapes and sizes drop in for dinner. Just when you think you've nearly cleared the room, more and bigger spiders arrive. Keep circling as you fire and try to avoid the webbing traps.

NEW AREA FOUND

"THE WIDOW'S COURT" (MAGIC)

When the last spider dies, the spear gate at the far end opens. Go seize the Skull Mask to complete the mission! Watch as the mask is placed in the Core of Light back at the Ruins. T-Bone reports that the Eternal Undead Source is hidden away in the Creepy Citadel. But first you need a Skeleton Key to get inside...

16

CADAVEROUS CRYPT

Talk to T-Bone and agree to descend the stairs into the Cadaverous Crypt. Your skeletal guide explains that the Skeleton Key is down here somewhere. But some of the crypt denizens are not happy about intruders!

	Treasure Chest
	Hat
	Soul Gem
	Story Scroll
	Legendary Item
—	Direct path from Start to Goal
—	Optional paths for bonus items

OBJECTIVE
FIND THE SKELETON KEY

ELEMENTAL GATES
TECH
EARTH

AREAS TO FIND
THE CATACOMBS
THE EVERSHIFTING HALL
MAZE OF SKULLS
THE SHRINE OF THE UNLIVING

NEW ENEMIES

RHU-BABIES

ROTTING ROBBIE

BONE 'N' ARROW

UNDEAD SPELL PUNK

RHU-BARB

COLLECTIONS

SOUL GEMS

**Skull Shield
(Hex)**

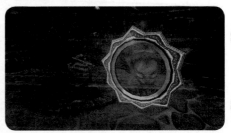

**Infinite Ammo
(Trigger Happy)**

LEGENDARY TREASURE

Golden Randomizer

HATS

Bone Head

Crown of Light

STORY SCROLLS

Life and Undeath

MISSION GUIDE

This first zone is The Catacombs. Step forward to face a pair of red Rhu-Babies. Beware their razor-sharp pincers at close range! Since they're "babies," they go down easy, but they tend to travel in packs. And you can bet they have some angry "parents" elsewhere in the crypt.

NEW AREA FOUND

"THE CATACOMBS" (FIRE)

BLAST OPEN THE WALLS

When the area is clear, approach the cannon **(1)**. Without moving it, fire to knock down the wall on the right. Enter the newly accessible room and clear out all the Spider Swarmers and the Spider Spitters that spawn them. Grab the Soul Gem that unlocks the "Skull Shield" power for the Undead Skylander named Hex.

Return to the cannon, use the nearby lever to swivel the big gun once—it turns 90 degrees— and blast open the far wall. A new foe, the Rotting Robbie, staggers into view. Note that the onscreen text tells you Robbies are vulnerable to fire (you can use a Fire Skylander or a candlestick). And cannons! So fire the cannon a second time. The second shot clears out any Rotting Robbies up the hall.

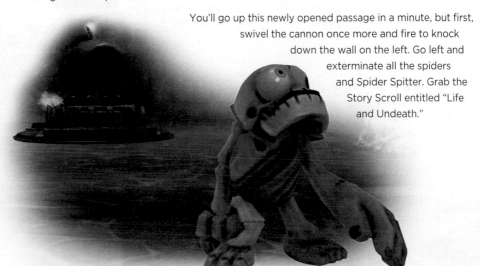

You'll go up this newly opened passage in a minute, but first, swivel the cannon once more and fire to knock down the wall on the left. Go left and exterminate all the spiders and Spider Spitter. Grab the Story Scroll entitled "Life and Undeath."

171

Now you're ready to move deeper into the crypt. Head up the open passage into the next corridor (2) to meet yet another new foe, the skeletal archer known as the Bone 'n' Arrow. These frightening fellows reload and aim somewhat slowly, but then they fire three arrows in quick succession that inflict major damage. Individually, the archers aren't very sturdy, but several of them pop out of coffins in the walls as you move up the corridor, pitting you against an entire platoon. Dash in close and hammer them with relentless melee attacks.

Continue to the corridor's end and turn right to reach a block puzzle **(3)**. This one is simple—just push blocks into the floor gaps so you can cross over and continue down the hall. Soon you run into an Undead Spell Punk **(4)** who can cast a purple glyph on the ground and conjure up a hulking Rhu-Barb, the larger "parental" version of the Rhu-Babies you faced earlier.

SPELL SHRINK

When you eliminate an Undead Spell Punk, any of the big Rhu-Barb minions he created will automatically shrink down into a Rhu-Babies!

Chase the Punk to the right as he tries to flee. The gate slams shut behind you! (You can't avoid this.) This is a new zone, The Evershifting Hall, and the name is apt. Wipe out all the enemies in this area—the next gate to the right automatically opens.

"THE EVERSHIFTING HALL" (UNDEAD)

Follow the new passage around the corner and down the stairs **(5)**; this is a different area of The Catacombs (where Fire is strongest), and a host of enemies are waiting for you. In particular, another Undead Spell Punk hides on the other side of a breakable wall to the left, conjuring up Rhu-Barbs. Smash through the wall and nail the Punk; you find a nice Treasure Chest as well. Then fight your way into the next alcove to nab the Soul Gem. This one unlocks the "Infinite Hellfire" power for Trigger Happy.

When you finish clearing enemies from this area, the next gate opens. Go downstairs to find a cannon facing the wrong way—the wall you want to blast open is behind it! Push the cannon along the track to the rotating platform **(6)** and then use the lever twice to swivel the gun 180 degrees. Now push the cannon back up the track and fire it to smash open the wall. Proceed to the elemental gate **(7)**.

ELEMENTAL GATE: TECH

Use a Tech Skylander to unlock the gate and cross the bridge to the teleport pad in a new zone, Maze of Skulls. Switch to your fastest Skylander and get ready to move fast—your destination has a 1:20 time limit! Use the pad to zap into a dank, dingy maze **(8)** filled with Bone 'n' Arrow archers, impaling spear traps, and collectible skulls.

NEW AREA FOUND
"MAZE OF SKULLS" (TECH)

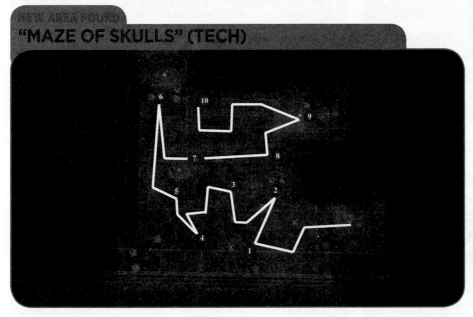

An onscreen timer appears, counting down from 1:20. Your goal is to collect 10 of the 12 skulls in the area. (See the overhead shot for the best route.) If you don't get ten skulls before the timer runs out, you simply zap back to the starting platform where you can give it another try. When you grab the tenth skull you automatically teleport back to the platform where you started: a hatbox now sits there. Shake it open to acquire the Crown of Light.

Exit the elemental gate and step on the nearby floor button **(9)** to open two more doors **(10)** just up the stairs. Go through those doors to face a spider/skeleton ambush. Wipe out all the attackers to open the door into the next corridor **(11)**.

Here you find two destructible walls blocking further passage. Knock down the one to the right first. It leads you to another elemental gate **(12)**.

ELEMENTAL GATE: EARTH

Use an Earth Skylander to unlock the gate and cross the bridge to the teleport pad. Switch to your fastest Skylander and get ready to hustle through a maze **(8)** configured exactly the same as the one you just visited via the Tech elemental gate, although you start in the opposite corner **(13)** and your camera view is reversed! (See the overhead shot.) This time the maze features Undead Spell Punks, Rhu-Barbs and Rhu-Babies along with the impaling spear traps and breakable walls.

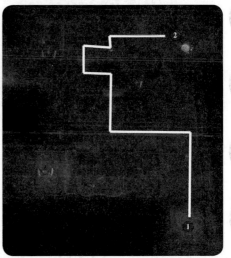

Your simple goal is to reach the teleport pad in the upper right corner of the map—no time limit this time. The pad zaps you back to the starting platform where two rewards await your return: a Treasure Chest and another hatbox. Shake both open to get loot and the Bone Head.

BLAST OPEN MORE WALLS

Exit the elemental gate and proceed up the stairs to the destructible wall. Smash through to find another cannon on a track. Push the cannon three times; it won't go any farther

because the rotating platform isn't aligned with the track. But you can blast the wall open on the left to gain access to a lever **(15)**. Squash all the enemies guarding the lever then pull it once to align the rotating platform with the track.

Now you can push the cannon four more times until the second rotating platform stops it. Blow open the next wall on the left to find another lever **(16)** in the room beyond; use it to align the rotating platform with the tracks. Finally, push the cannon all the way to the end of the track and blow open the last wall on the left. Watch the brief cinematic as four interior walls drop, leaving an open path to the key **(18)** you need!

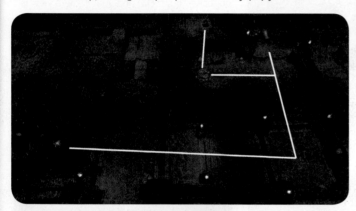

Before you seek the key, head right to find a teleport pad **(17)** hidden under a pile of bones. Use the pad to reach a legendary treasure, the Golden Randomizer.

En route to the key you get ambushed several times. Fight off the foes and proceed to the key **(18)**. Use it to unlock the door **(19)** across the main hall. Enter to find another cannon, some tracks, a rotating platform **(20)**, and three destructible walls (circled in the overhead shot).

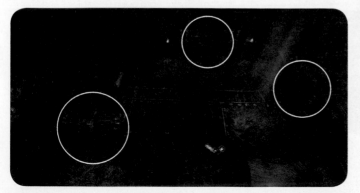

Take the following steps:

- Push the cannon onto the rotating platform and fire a shot to knock down the back wall. Grab the loot!
- Use the lever twice to swivel the cannon 180 degrees.
- Push the cannon back to where it started and blast open the wall to the Treasure Chest. Grab the chest!
- Push the cannon back onto the rotating platform and swivel it once to face the door to the right.
- Blast down the door and exit through the new opening.

There's another cannon in the next room. Take the following steps:

- Fire the cannon right away to knock down the door ahead.
- Push the cannon into the next room. It stops at a rotating platform **(21)**.
- Use the lever once to align the platform with the tracks then push the cannon onto the platform.
- Use the lever swivel the gun toward the raised drawbridge.
- Fire the cannon to knock down the bridge.

FIND THE SKELETON KEY

Cross the bridge into the arena-like chamber called The Shrine of the Unliving **(22)**. Time to fight! Waves of enemies come at you here. After you clear the first bunch and chase down the Undead Spell Punk as he retreats up the stairs, you find that another hostile wave arrives when you return to the arena.

"THE SHRINE OF THE UNLIVING" (UNDEAD)

Eliminate all foes to trigger open the final door to the left. Go through to find the Skeleton Key. You automatically deliver it to T-Bone (who uses it in an unusual manner) and thus complete the mission.

17

CREEPY CITADEL

Talk to T-Bone and agree to descend the stairs to the Creepy Citadel. When you arrive, T-Bone really uses his head to get you past the outer gate. He also gives you a rundown of your tasks: Get into the castle via the main gate, fight your way over to a side gateway, and use it to find the Eternal Undead Source.

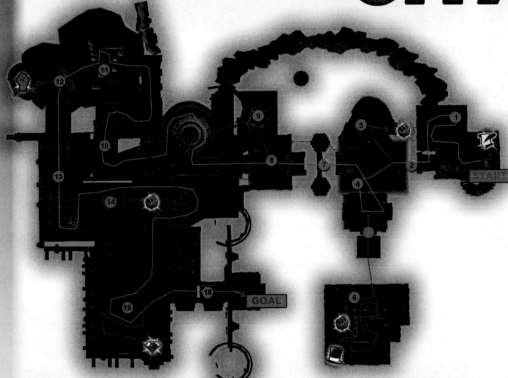

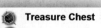	**Treasure Chest**
	Hat
	Soul Gem
	Story Scroll
	Legendary Item
——	Direct path from Start to Goal
——	Optional paths for bonus items

OBJECTIVES
ENTER THE CASTLE
COLLECT THE ETERNAL UNDEAD SOURCE

ELEMENTAL GATES
AIR

AREAS TO FIND
SKELETON GATE
TOMB OF STONES
MAIN GATE
BOX GOBLIN SWAMP
THE GALLERY
THE GRAND BALLROOM
THE UNDEAD GATEWAY

NEW ENEMIES

SHADOW KNIGHT

DARK KNIGHT MINION

DARK IMP MINION

DARK WITCH MINION

COLLECTIONS

SOUL GEMS

Healing Rainbow
(Whirlwind)

LEGENDARY TREASURE

Doom's Rook

HATS

Rocket Hair

STORY SCROLLS

Skylanders' battle cry

When Skylanders travel through a portal it is customary for them to yell out a fierce battle cry when they appear. In fact, each year there is a great contest to see whose Cry is loudest, the most frightening and the best at making milk shoot out of other people's noses.

Skylander's battle cry

MISSION GUIDE

Grab the Story Scroll (entitled "Skylanders' Battle Cry") to the right of the gate T-Bone just opened before you enter the first zone, Skeleton Gate. Then go down the ramp to the crystal puzzle.

NEW AREA FOUND
"SKELETON GATE" (WATER)

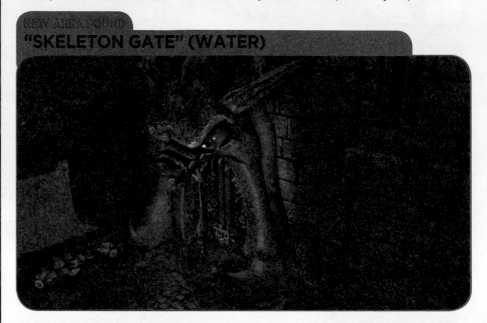

REDIRECT THE BEAM

You want to direct the energy beam to the crystal at the bottom of the ramp. Step on the floor button to reverse the blocks, push the only movable crystal right once and back twice, and then use the lever four times to rotate the beam to that crystal. The beam ends up hitting the crystal that lowers the drawbridge **(2)**.

Cross the now-lowered bridge and veer right down the collapsed floor to the teleport pad **(3)**. Use the pad to zap across to the Treasure Chest, then teleport up to the plaza.

There, use the lever to swivel the rotating crystal once so it shoots into the crystal on the next platform. Use the nearby teleport pad **(4)** to reach that platform. Now take the following steps to solve the crystal puzzle:

- **Step on the floor button in the back right corner to lower blocks, revealing a new floor button near the lever.**
- **Step on the new floor button to lower the block next to the movable crystal.**
- **Push the movable crystal twice to the right—as far as it can go.**
- **Step on the floor button by the lever to change the blocks again.**
- **Push the movable crystal forward (toward the camera) once, then right once. Now it's pointing at the correct crystal (the one aiming off to the right).**
- **Use the lever twice to swivel the rotating crystal.**

The energy beam gets redirected to a crystal that powers the big drawbridge **(7)** that leads to the castle gate. The bridge lowers. Nice work! But before you head for the castle, approach the elemental gate **(5)** at the end of the platform you're on now.

ELEMENTAL GATE: AIR

Use an Air Skylander to unlock the gate and use the whirlwind to transport over to the next platform, the Tomb of Stones. Refer to the overhead shot for the following steps:

"TOMB OF STONES" (AIR)

- **Run down the narrow corridor (avoiding the impaling spear traps) and push the only movable block at 1.**
- **Go step on the floor button at 2 to lower the block sets at 3 and 4.**
- **Grab a bomb at 5 push the block at 6, then stop on the button which lowers the block at 7. Run to 8 with the bomb and demolish the wall.**
- **Move the block at 9 and step on the disc, which drops the blocks at 10 into the floor.**
- **Run back to 5 for another bomb, carry it to 11 to destroy the wall. Run up the ramp, collect the treasure chest and use the bounce pad at 12 to reach 13.**
- **Use the disc at 14 to drop the block at 15, which reveals a bounce pad. Use the bounce pad to reach the hatbox. Shake it open to get the Rocket Hair.**
- **Walk back over the lowered blocks to reach the whirlwind and exit the Tomb of Stones!**

Exit the elemental gate and use the teleport pad to get back to the main platform.

ENTER THE CASTLE

Cross the drawbridge **(7)** to a new zone, the Main Gate **(8)**, where a new foe stands guard: the Shadow Knight. This powerful warrior moves slowly but when he thrusts his broadsword downward, sparkling waves of energy radiate out from the strike. These hits inflict great damage, so get back quickly when you see his sword descend!

"MAIN GATE" (WATER)

When you finally defeat the Knight, the coast is clear to the Lock Puzzle on the castle gate. Turn the Lock Puzzle in the following order: 2L, 2R, L, 5R, 9L, 3R. The Wii solution is R ,2L, 3R, 2L, 2R.

Solving the puzzle completes the first mission objective, "Enter the Castle." But note that you can bypass both the Lock Puzzle and the painful swinging blades of the castle entry hall. While using a Water Skylander, veer to the right of the front gate and jump into the whirlpool **(9)**. This transports you to a pool inside the castle just past the entry hall. However, the first objective doesn't check off in your Objectives list if you enter the castle this way.

CROSS THE GOBLIN SWAMP

Fight off the enemies and continue up into the castle. Around the first corner you run into some spiders including a Gargantula guarding a spear gate **(10)**. Wipe them out so the gate retracts, and continue working your way down to the Box Goblin Swamp **(11)**. The Box Goblins who give their name to the passage are not hostile, but they are passive aggressive—they won't just move for you.

"BOX GOBLIN SWAMP" (WATER)

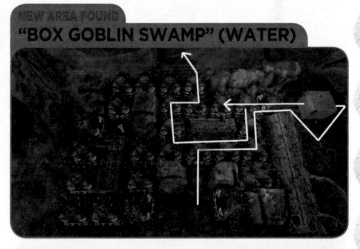

You can see the path through the goblins on the overhead shot, but here's a step-by-step guide:

- **Step on the first floor button to reveal two more buttons.**
- **Go step on the next button to the right. This reveals a square pressure pad. Your Skylander is too light to depress the pad, however.**
- **Push the block from the far right onto the pressure pad. This reveals another floor button.**
- **Step on the newly revealed button to clear the path out of the swamp.**

Two huge Gargantulas defend the next island **(12)**. Defeat them to open the exit gate and then grab the Soul Gem. This gem unlocks the "Healing Rainbow" power for the Air Skylander named Whirlwind.

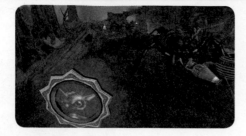

FIND THE BALLROOM

Now proceed through the swinging blades of the long stone walkway **(13)** as you enter a new zone, The Gallery. Work your way up past the unusual paintings until you reach a chamber **(14)** that triggers an ambush: gates rise up and trap you in with Shadow Knights and Moon Widows. Once you clear the room, the gates up ahead reopen.

NEW AREA FOUND
"THE GALLERY" (UNDEAD)

Keep battling up the corridor, snatching the Treasure Chest from the alcove at the top of the stone ramp. Move carefully down another swinging-blade corridor past a pair of Shadow Knights into The Grand Ballroom **(15)**.

NEW AREA FOUND
"THE GRAND BALLROOM"

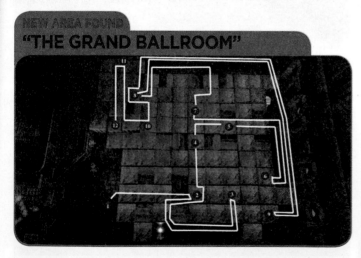

Here you face a really big block puzzle. But the path is easier than it looks. The basic pattern is to move from floor button to floor button, stepping on each successive button (from 1 to 12 on the map above) revealed without stepping on any you've already depressed.

When you reach the final button at 12, the energy beam opens the room's exit gate. Backtrack to button 9 without touching any other button and press it again to open the path to the legendary treasure, the Doom's Rook.

Fight down the red-lit corridor **(16)** until every foe is vanquished to open the gate to the Undead Gateway and step into the glowing circle to be whisked away to a combat arena.

DEFEAT THE MINIONS OF KAOS

Guess who appears? Yes, it's Kaos and his minions again. This battle follows the usual Kaos pattern—you face a sequence of three dark minions, but Kaos casts special spell attacks between each minion's appearance. At the end, all three minions attack at once.

NEW AREA FOUND
"THE UNDEAD GATEWAY"

The first evil minion is an undead Dark Knight. This foe's attack pattern is simple: he takes two huge swings with his sword and then unleashes a spinning attack. When you see the sword swing, get ready to dodge the spinning dash! Counterattack as he recovers from the spin.

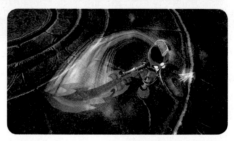

WII BOSSES

On the Wii, you face the Dark Imp before the Dark Knight but the strategy to defeat them is the same.

Next, Kaos uncorks his Evil Undead Spell of Destruction, a series of energy beams that start out a benign white then switch to a lethal red. During the white phase, you can discern the pattern as it develops and then quickly step into a safe space before the beams turn red.

Kaos' second evil undead minion is a cackling Dark Imp who suddenly transforms into a huge green skull and makes three quick chomping dashes. After these three attacks he stops to cackle, so nail him during this interlude of self-satisfied amusement.

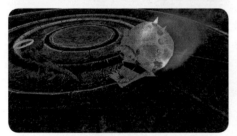

After another interlude of white/red beams summoned by Kaos, a third minion arrives. The Dark Witch fires three deadly dark-matter bolts then summons a bone cage for protection as she flings explosive skulls at you. The skulls drop fast, so you must stay on your toes in order to dodge them. Destroy the cage, bone by bone, to flush out the witch and terminate her.

After one more interlude of the beam spell, Kaos drops all three minions into the arena at once. He also tosses in an occasional Undead spell to keep things interesting. This is a very tough fight, so it helps to have plenty of healthy, upgraded, and leveled-up Skylanders to swap on the *Portal of Power* when your combatants get drained. When you finally win the battle, Kaos gives up his beloved Eternal Undead Source.

BACK AT THE RUINS: BLAST OPEN THE MINE!

Once the Undead source is in place, a new area with a train and railroad tracks opens up at the Ruins. Diggs the Molekin explains that the tracks lead into a mining complex where his people were searching for the Crucible of the Ages until a terrible cave-in. Grab the Winged Sapphire as soon as you regain control of your Skylander.

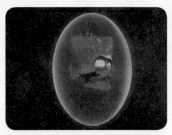

Run down to the beach and grab a bomb from the Clam-tron 4000. Then hustle along the nearby train tracks and toss it at the blocked cave mouth. Now you have access to the Molekin Mine!

Run a second bomb up the ramp (follow the train tracks) and blow up the loose rocks blocking a cave entrance north of the engine's location. Collect the Winged Sapphire you find there. Run a third bomb up the train tracks and toss it into the geyser to disable its steam production. Jump down the hole and collect the Winged Sapphire you find there. For a third Winged Sapphire, get the oil can from the beach and oil the train at the top of the tracks.

18 MOLEKIN MINE

Talk to Diggs by the steam train and agree to ride down into the Molekin Mine. You meet Blobbers, one of the townsfolk you saved back on Shattered Island. He explains that once the Molekin miners found the ancient relic known as the Crucible of the Ages, something triggered a cave-in. Now the miners are trapped!

 Treasure Chest

 Hat

Soul Gem

 Story Scroll

Legendary Item

— Direct path from Start to Goal

— Optional paths for bonus items

OBJECTIVES
RESCUE ALL 7 MOLEKIN MINERS

ROLL MOLEKIN IN CART TO SAFETY

ELEMENTAL GATE
TECH

AREAS TO FIND
ACCESS TUNNEL VIN

THE SECRET CLAIM

THE UNDERGROUND LAKE

THE CRYSTAL GROVE

NEW ENEMIES
You saw the Flame Imp and Lava King earlier, in the Troll Warehouse of Chapter 12, but only if you explored beyond the Fire elemental gate in that chapter. They're listed here in case you missed them then.

FLAME IMP   ROCKER WALKER   LAVA KING

COLLECTIONS

SOUL GEMS

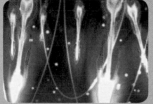

Haunted Ally (Cynder)

Super Volley Shot (Flameslinger)

LEGENDARY TREASURE

Golden Links

HATS

Miner Hat

STORY SCROLLS

Core of Light Origin

Who created the Core of Light? None other than the Benevolent Ancients who vanished a thousand years ago. Their great machine filled the skies with Light and kept the Darkness at bay. At least until that fool Kaos, destroyed it. Now the Darkness spreads.

Core of Light Origin

MISSION GUIDE

A total of seven Molekin Miners must be rescued. Blast through the debris blocking the tracks; use either your Earth Skylander's attack or the miner's pick floating near Blobbers. (Look for valuable gems and gold nuggets as you smash through any debris in the mines.) Move down the tracks to see a Miner **(1)** terrorized by Flame Imps. Wipe out the little monsters and walk through the miner to rescue him. One down, six to go!

NEW AREA FOUND

"ACCESS TUNNEL VIN" (EARTH)

IMP INTRODUCTION

Flame Imps were first encountered beyond the Fire elemental gate back in Chapter 12: Troll Warehouse. But if you didn't explore that area, this is your first encounter with them.

SAVE THE MINERS

Continue down the tunnel to face a Rocker Walker, cousin of the lava-spewing Rock Walkers you met in Chapter 9: Stonetown. This fellow spews lava too, but it comes out as fiery cannonballs that travel fast and hit hard from long range.

He chortles for a few seconds between lava balls, so get in your shots then.

Find the big rockslide on the right wall and smash through to rescue another Miner **(2)** from a trio of nasty Flame Imps dancing around him. (Two down, five to go.) Bash the three barrels and veer down the side passage to the elemental gate **(3)**.

ELEMENTAL GATE: TECH

Use a Tech Skylander to unlock the gate then proceed across the bridge into a new zone, The Secret Claim. Use the miner's pick to hack through the next cave-in to reach a cannon **(4)** on a sidetrack. The big gun is pointed at some blocks and crystal formations.

NEW AREA FOUND
"THE SECRET CLAIM" (TECH)

Now you want to use the cannon to help you reach the hatbox behind the blocks and crystals. Your goal is to move the blocks so that you can shatter the crystals with cannonballs. Refer to the first overhead shot and do the following:

- Push the block at 1 twice to the left.

- Push the cannon at 2 once to the left.
- Push the blocks at 3 and 4 once each toward the track.
- Push the blocks at 5 and 6 once each toward the back wall.
- Fire the cannon to destroy the crystals at 7.

Now you want to blast the other two crystals. Check out the next overhead shot to see the next steps:

- Push the block at 1 forward once and then right.

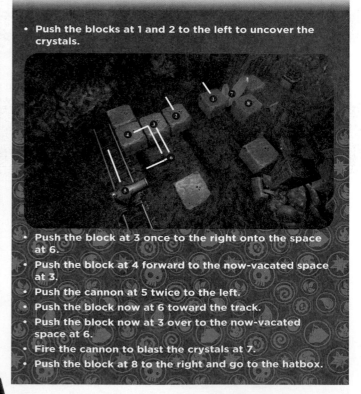

- Push the block at 2 once to the right to uncover the crystals.
- Push the cannon at 3 once to the right.
- Fire the cannon to shatter the crystals at 4.

Just one more crystal formation left to destroy. Refer to the third overhead shot and make the following moves:

- Push the blocks at 1 and 2 to the left to uncover the crystals.

- Push the block at 3 once to the right onto the space at 6.
- Push the block at 4 forward to the now-vacated space at 3.
- Push the cannon at 5 twice to the left.
- Push the block now at 6 toward the track.
- Push the block now at 3 over to the now-vacated space at 6.
- Fire the cannon to blast the crystals at 7.
- Push the block at 8 to the right and go to the hatbox.

Shake the hatbox to get the Miner Hat, a useful addition to your collection. Equip it if you want, and then exit the area via the elemental gate.

Before you return to the main tunnel, continue down the narrow shaft to see the fan **(7)** and the Legendary Treasure just beyond it. The fan's exhaust is too strong—you can't get past it to the treasure, but there's a way to turn off the fan.

BEAT THE FAN TIMER!

Find the rockslide blocking the narrow passage on the left of the main tunnel **(5)**. Hammer through that blockage and the next, smaller one to reach a cave with a floor button **(6)**. Switch to your fastest Skylander then step on the button to see the big fan deactivated **(7)**.

The fan deactivates for just 60 seconds—an onscreen timer marks the countdown. Hurry! Fly back to the narrow shaft and slip past the fan **(7)** to grab the Golden Links.

SAVE MORE MINERS

Return to the main tunnel and continue deeper until you face a frontal assault by Rocker Walkers and Flame Imps at the wooden bridge over The Underground Lake, an area strong in the Water element. Defeat the enemies and go down the ramp to the cannon. Push the block left then forward; push the cannon to the right and blast through the crystals blocking the passage. Go up the newly opened passage and save the Miner **(9)**.

NEW AREA FOUND
"THE UNDERGROUND LAKE" (WATER)

Return to the bridge and continue into the mine. A big Lava King spawns Lava Imps and chases you with his arms spewing like flamethrowers. Keep picking off the Imps and don't let the big guy get close! When these foes fall, use the pick to smash through the fallen rock ahead **(10)**.

See the huge mechanical monster hammering rocks just to the right? Don't let it hit you! This excavator machine packs a wallop with massive damage per hit. Knock it out carefully then continue into the blocked room to save the Miner **(11)** from the Flame Imps. Hack through the rocks to another Miner **(12)** and a Story Scroll entitled "Core of Light Origin." That's five Miners saved, and only two left!

TZO CRYSTALS

Huge purplish Tzo Crystals sprout in several passages in the mine. Each location is marked with a bomb icon on the ground; each crystal formation also encases a valuable gem. When you finally gain access to bombs, use them to shatter the Tzo Crystals and gather the gems.

Now continue to the end of the main tunnel where a Molekin survivor **(13)** waits by a mining cart and a locked door with a bomb inside. Clearly you need a key, so start looking.

FIND THE KEY

Turn left and hammer your way through rocks to another excavator machine. Take him out and continue your own excavating until you reach another Miner **(14)** held captive by Flame Imps. Liberate him and move on. Only one more to go!

Bash through the next blocked passage **(15)** and move down the slope to find three special items in the Underground Lake area **(16)**. A Treasure Chest is tucked in a rock alcove blocked by a small pile of debris; another Treasure Chest is in a small room blocked by a few barrels; and a Soul Gem sits on a small island on the lake. (This gem unlocks the "Haunted Ally" power for Cynder.)

After you collect this cornucopia of goodies, go back up the slope from the lake, turn left, and enter the room below **(17)** to find the last trapped Miner, plus a chattering Hob 'n' Yaro with the key you seek and a surly Lava King with an apparent craving for roast Skylander. Take out the big monster and nail the thief with ranged shots to get the key.

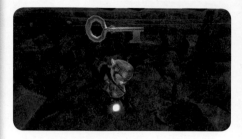

Now liberate the Miner to mark completion of your first objective—all seven trapped Miners have been rescued. This triggers a quick scene: the Molekin survivor reports that he has the Crucible for the Ages, but he can't walk and needs help out of the mine! Then he grabs the object and crawls into the nearby mining cart.

GET THE GEM IN CRYSTAL GROVE

Your final main objective is to save the Molekin and the Crucible by pushing the minecar out of the mine. Before you do that, however, use the key you acquired from the Hob 'n' Yaro to open the locked gate **(13)**. Now you can toss bombs at the two Tzo Crystal formations in passages lining the main tunnel, and collect the valuable gems encased in them. You can also collect a second Soul Gem.

Run a bomb up to the small, crystal-choked passage **(18)** to gain access to the last unexplored area, The Crystal Grove. Your goal here is to use the outside pair of cannons to blast crystals so that you can move a third cannon. Push blocks around and move the cannons on their tracks to get shooting angles at crystals.

"THE CRYSTAL GROVE" (WATER)

Eventually you can push out the two blocks that box in the cannon at the far end of the grove. Then you can use that cannon to destroy the crystal blocking access to the Soul Gem, which unlocks the "Super Volley Shot" power for the Fire Skylander named Flame Slinger. Look for a Treasure Chest as well.

ROLL THE MOLEKIN TO SAFETY

Now return to the Molekin with the Crucible in the mining cart. Move your Skylander into the back of the cart to push it. Keep pushing until you reach Blobbers and the other rescued Miners to complete the mission. Blobbers reports that the seismic activity has opened up some new passages and tracks deeper in the Molekin Mine.

BACK AT THE RUINS

With the addition of the Crucible of the Ages, the Core of Light is nearly complete. This is good news for your side, but not so good for Kaos, who sends Glumshanks on a little errand to the Lava Lakes while the evil master seeks to secure the final piece, the Eternal Fire Source.

19

LAVA LAKES RAILWAY

Talk to Diggs and agree to ride the train to the Lava Lakes. When you arrive at the entrance, Diggs points out that the way ahead is blocked. You need to find levers to switch the tracks so your train can continue the journey.

	Treasure Chest
	Hat
	Soul Gem
	Story Scroll
	Legendary Item
—	Direct path from Start to Goal
—	Optional paths for bonus items

OBJECTIVES

SET EACH OF THE TRACK SWITCHES

REPAIR THE TRAIN TRACKS

FIND THE ETERNAL FIRE SOURCE

ELEMENTAL GATE

FIRE

AREAS TO FIND

THE MOLEKIN MINES

CRYSTAL GROTTOES

LAVA LAGOON

FIREY DEPTHS

THE FIRE SOURCE

NEW ENEMIES

FIRE SPELL PUNK

DARK PYRO ARCHER

DARK PHOENIX DRAGON

DARK EVIL ERUPTOR

MISSION GUIDE

As you step away from the train, a new foe appears: the Fire Spell Punk. This Punk's magic trick: spawn an explosive barrel, float away from it, and then shoot out a flaming "fuse" that detonates the barrel. Avoid these barrels, obviously, and try to hit the Punk as he lays the fuse. Watch out for the pack of Flame Imps just on the other side of the destructible wall, too. When the area is clear, grab the miner's pick **(1)** from the side alcove.

COLLECTIONS

SOUL GEMS

Mega Magma Balls (Eruptor)

LEGENDARY TREASURE

Fiord's Jetty

HATS

Lil Devil

STORY SCROLLS

Floating islands

Skylands is an endless sea of clouds in which float rocky islands too numerous to count. Some of these islands are as large as an entire kingdom while others overflow with salty seas or are swollen with fiery volcanoes. Each is unique.

Floating islands

"THE MOLEKIN MINES" (UNDEAD)

SET THE TRACK SWITCHES

Follow the main tracks to the side passage blocked by a cave-in with a spider web hanging in front. Pick through the rocks and follow the passage around to the rail switch **(2)**. Throw the switch to align the tracks then hop down to the train to trigger a scene: the engine steams forward to the next switching platform. Diggs says the raised gate up ahead leads to the Crystal Grottoes; he suggests looking for another lever.

At the track intersection, bust through the debris on the left side to clear the side track to the cannon **(3)**. Push the cannon forward to the main track and fire it to blast open the opposite wall and reveal the switch lever in an alcove **(4)**. But then fire the cannon a second time to knock down the alcove's back wall, revealing a hidden room.

Pull the lever to rotate the track and open the gate ahead. Then enter the back room where another Fire Spell Punk pops up to stop you. Eliminate him and grab the loot including a Soul Gem that unlocks the "Mega Magma Balls" power for the Fire Skylander named Eruptor.

OPEN THE LAVA LAKES GATE

Return to the train engine to trigger another scene: the train moves further down the tracks to a closed gate **(5)**. The lever that opens it is on the other side of a big Tzo Crystal formation next to the engine; you need a bomb to blast through it.

"CRYSTAL GROTTOES"

Backtrack to the side tunnel leading left to find the bomb you need **(6)**. Continue past the bomb alcove up another narrow passage to find a Treasure Chest. Then grab a bomb and run it back to the Tzo Crystal formation to blast your way to the lever. Pull the lever to open the gate to the fiery lava lakes.

Before you return to the train engine, explore up the side passage from the lever. You find a big cavern with another Treasure Chest and a legendary treasure, the Fiord's Jetty. Now return to the engine to ride into the volcanic lakes below.

REPAIR THE TRACK ROUTE

Watch as Diggs stops the train **(8)** before a stretch of track that's been sabotaged. (You also catch a glimpse of the saboteur: Glumshanks!) Now your task is to use the blocks to fill in the gaps in the track route. Then Diggs will repair the railroad track itself.

Look to the left of the train for the Story Scroll, "Floating Islands." Walk to the blocks and push the first one to the left twice and then back once so it aligns with the other three blocks (as in the screenshot). Walk up onto the track and use this four-block bridge to reach the Treasure Chest on the small plateau. Then hop down to push more blocks.

Refer to the first overhead shot and take the following steps in the first block area:

- Push the blocks at 1 and 2 into the gap.
- Push the block at 3 left once and then three times forward (away from the camera) until it drops in the gap at 9 directly under the track route.
- Push the block at 4 forward twice to the spot at 5 so you can get to the other side of the track.
- Push the block at 6 twice to the left until it drops into the gap at 7.
- Push the block at 8 three times to the right and once toward the camera so it bridges the track route at 9.
- Push the block at 10 forward once so it falls into the gap.
- Push the block now at 5 back to where it started at 4 to complete the track route repair in this area.
- Push the block at 11 forward once, left once, and forward again to bridge the track route at 12.

Head back up the slope to Diggs and the train. From there, walk down the track to the next sabotaged section **(9)**. Refer to the second overhead shot and do the following:

- Push the blocks at 1 and 2 forward to align under the track route.
- Push the block at 3 forward into the gap.
- Push the block at 4 twice toward the camera and then to the right once into the single gap at 5.
- Push the block at 6 once to the right and then back into the gap at 7.
- Push the block at 8 twice to the right and forward three times over the block you just pushed to 7.
- Walk up the track and push the block at 9 down into the gap to complete the track route repair.

This final move triggers a cinematic: Diggs fixes the tracks and you ride to the end of the mining track **(10).** You end up on a high plateau overlooking the next area, the spectacular Lava Lagoon.

NEW AREA FOUND
"LAVA LAGOON" (FIRE)

ELEMENTAL GATE: FIRE

Fight your way along the route until the paths split **(11)** and veer right to the elemental gate. Use a Fire Skylander to unlock the elemental gate and enter a new zone, the Firey Depths.

NEW AREA FOUND
"FIREY DEPTHS" (FIRE)

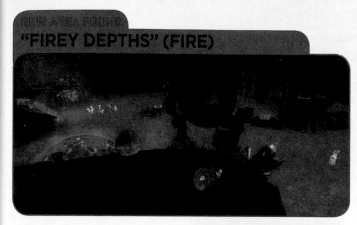

Follow the walkway to the intersection and go right first. Use the bounce pads to hop up to a pair of walk-bridges. Cross the gaps in the bridges using the rising and falling platforms. (You can ride them down first and collect a few extra gems, if you want.) Collect valuable gems

on the topmost platform then use the teleport pad to return to the elemental gate.

Go to the intersection again and turn left. If you're using a Fire Skylander he can ignore all the bounce pads and just walk across the lava to the small island with a hatbox. Use the last bounce pad to hop up onto the island then shake open the box to acquire the Lil Devil hat. Use the teleport pad

to return to the elemental gate then exit the Firey Depths.

Continue along the path to the left. Watch out for globs of lava bouncing over the path—time your run to get past them! Extinguish the Lava King on the next platform to the right to open the last gate **(12)** and cross to the final island, The Fire Source. Guess who's waiting for you again?

NEW AREA FOUND
"THE FIRE SOURCE"

DEFEAT THE MINIONS OF KAOS

You should be familiar with the Kaos "boss fight" pattern by now: three minions with spell attacks between, then all three minions together at the end. The first minion is a Dark Pyro Archer who slings five arrows in a row at you then dashes to a new location. After you defeat him, Kaos casts a Fire spell that drops firebombs onto yellow targeting reticles that appear all over the platform. Simply run away from the reticles.

The second minion is the Dark Phoenix Dragon. This creature breathes a deadly stream of fire. It can teleport right next to you and leave a burning disc under your feet too. Keep

moving! When the dragon falls, be ready for another round of Fire spells from Kaos.

The third minion is the Dark Evil Eruptor. This flamebroiled monster tosses magma bombs then suddenly "erupts" in a scalding pool of lava. Keep your distance from this fellow and nail him from afar, if you can.

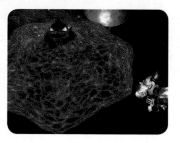

If you survive more Fire spells and a final visit from all three minions at once, Kaos gives up the Eternal Fire Source, but swears he won't hand over the final piece of the Core of Light.

BACK AT THE RUINS

After you watch the Fire source take its place in the Core, you end up on an island off the Ruins facing a massive statue named the Weapon Master. Talk to him once to learn about the Quicksilver Vault.

20
QUICKSILVER VAULT

Talk to the Weapon Master and agree to cross the chain to the Quicksilver Vault. When you arrive, the Master explains that the Eternal Magic Source is the original source of all creations. Then he explains that you must prove your worth here.

GOAL

START

Legend

 Treasure Chest
 Hat
 Soul Gem
 Story Scroll
 Legendary Item
—— Direct path from Start to Goal
—— Optional paths for bonus items

OBJECTIVES

UNLOCK THE GATE TO THE VAULT

ACTIVATE THE VAULT BEAMS

FIND THE VIAL OF QUICK-SILVER

ELEMENTAL GATE

LIFE

AREAS TO FIND

SKELETON GATE
MAIN GATE
DIMENSIONAL RIFTS
THE SCION OF EARTH
THE GRAND BALLROOM

NEW ENEMIES

ARKEYAN BLASTER

GNASHER

MAGIC SPELL PUNK

ARKEYAN DEFENDER

ARKEYAN ULTRON

COLLECTIONS

SOUL GEMS

Digestive Detonation (Wrecking Ball)

LEGENDARY TREASURE

Rollerskates

HATS

Unicorn Hat

STORY SCROLLS

Skylanders

Skylanders have a bond with their Portal Masters that is unbreakable, but they are not slaves. They have chosen to serve their Portal Master and do so eagerly. When Skylanders are defeated in battle, they instantly portal back home, where they can rest and heal.

Skylanders

MISSION GUIDE

You start out at the Skeleton Gate. Go down the ramp to the gate guarded by two Arkeyan Blasters. These weapons fire projectiles that float in a charged grid. If you step into them they explode and inflict damage. Take out the Blasters from a distance if you can. When they're destroyed, the gate behind them opens when you approach it.

NEW AREA FOUND

"SKELETON GATE" (AIR)

FIND THE KEY TO THE FIRST GATE

Step through to face a host of Gnashers, nasty blue imps that rush to give you a charged kick. Nail them before they get into close range to avoid damage. Take a quick left to find a lockbox **(2)** blocking the way to a Treasure Chest. To solve the Lock Puzzle, turn the lockbox in the following sequence: 4L, 3R, L, 7R, 2L, 5R, 2L.

Exit the alcove and head to the right. Smash through the destructible wall and continue to the right to meet your first Arkeyan Defender, a robotic fighter with a charged field that shields it from damage. When the Defender strikes, however, his shield drops, so launch your counterstrikes immediately after he swings his fearsome weapon. (It sticks in the ground for a few seconds, leaving the Defender vulnerable too.)

Further ahead you run into another Defender backed by three Blasters! Battle to the end of the walkway to find more Blasters guarding a key. Grab the key, retrace your route back, and use the key to open the locked gate **(4)**.

FIND THE KEY TO THE SECOND GATE

Go through the newly opened gate and take the first left to the lockbox. Solve the Lock Puzzle by turning the box in the following order: 3R, L, 6R, L, 3R, L, 3R. Shake open the Treasure Chest inside then exit the alcove.

Take out the Arkeyan Defenders on the next landing and turn the corner to face yet another ancient war machine, the Arkeyan Ultron **(5)**. This robotic warrior guards another locked gate, and wields a pair of bomb-launchers as appendages. First, he launches flights of guided bombs skyward, and then shoots blue tracking

beams from his eyes. If these eye-beams hit you, a red targeting beam locks on your position, and soon two flights of bombs drop right on your head in quick succession if you don't move fast!

When the Ultron finally falls, a teleport pad appears. First, nab the nearby Soul Gem. (This one unlocks the "Digestive Detonation" power for Wrecking Ball.) Then step on the pad to transport to another floating platform **(6)** in the Main Gate area.

NEW AREA FOUND
"MAIN GATE"

Waiting for you, unfortunately, is a Magic Spell Punk. This Punk conjures up floating, reanimated orbs that zing you with painful energy. You can't strike the orb so eliminate it by taking out the Punk.

Exit the platform by walking across the big chain links and defeat the Arkeyan Defenders on the next platform **(7)**. Grab the key, shake the goodies out of the Treasure Chest, and cross back over to the first platform **(6)**. Aha! A new teleport pad has appeared. Use it to transport to a platform crawling with Gnashers and another Magic Spell Punk **(8)**. When you clear that platform of foes, yet another teleport pad appears. Use it!

Once again, you arrive in the midst of hostile Arkeyan fighters, including another Ultron. Clear out the enemies to trigger the appearance another teleport pad. But this platform also features an elemental gate **(9)**.

So now you have a choice. You can use the teleport to go unlock the next gate **(10)**—the key should still be with you. Or you can explore beyond the elemental gate first. This walkthrough goes with the latter. (The key floats with you wherever you go, so don't worry about losing it if you don't use it right away.)

ELEMENTAL GATE: LIFE

Switch to a Life Skylander and unlock the elemental gate. Cross the bridge to the teleport pad on the next platform. This is a new zone called Dimensional Rifts. Use the pad to transport to a floating island **(11)**, one of four connected via moving blocks.

NEW AREA FOUND
"DIMENSIONAL RIFTS" (LIFE)

Here's the best route: Go first to the island on the right **(12)** and shake open the hatbox to get the Unicorn Hat. Then work your way across the moving blocks to reach the leftmost island **(13)** and step on its floor button. This opens the spear gate on the center island **(14)**. Work your way to that center island and collect a legendary treasure, the Rollerskates. Then use the teleport pad there to return to the Life elemental gate **(9)**.

Use the teleport next to the elemental gate to transport to the locked gate **(15)** and open it using the key you've been carrying. This triggers a quick glimpse of the Quicksilver Vault and the Weapon Master's instructions: align the three energy beams with the three seals to open the vault.

ALIGN THE BEAMS

Slide down the long chain beyond the unlocked gate to enter the next zone, The Scion of Earth, strong in the Magic element. Veer left and fight through a variety of foes then grab the Story Scroll entitled "Skylanders."

NEW AREA FOUND
"THE SCION OF EARTH" (LIFE)

Continue along the stone walkway and cross another length of massive chain links to a small platform with nothing but a teleport pad **(16)**. Use it!

FIRST BEAM

You end up on a platform with a crystal beam puzzle **(17)**. Here are the steps:

- Push the second block to the left.
- Push the first block forward (away from the camera) to connect the beam to the first crystal.
- Push the first crystal (the one receiving the beam now) twice to the left.
- Push the second crystal to the left.
- Push the rightmost block back toward the camera.
- Push the other block to the right.

This completes the circuit and the beam shoots down to one of the three vault seals. Here's what the arrangement looks like when you've made the full connection:

SECOND BEAM

Slide down the chain to the next crystal puzzle **(18)**. Take the following steps:

- Push the second movable block to the right.
- Push the first movable block forward (away from the camera).
- Push the first movable crystal (the one receiving the beam) twice to the right.
- Push the third movable box once forward (away from the camera).
- Push the second crystal to the right.
- Push the next box toward the camera.
- Push the rightmost box to the left.

This completes the circuit and the beam shoots down to another one of the three vault seals. Here's what the arrangement looks like when you've made the connection:

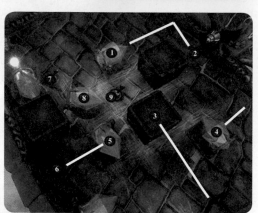

THIRD BEAM

Slide down the chain to the final crystal puzzle **(19)**. This solution is harder to describe so please refer to the numbers on the overhead shot for the following steps:

- Push the crystal at 1 forward twice and to the right once. Now it sits at 2, almost nose to nose with the target crystal.
- Push the box at 3 twice to the right.
- Push the crystal at 4 once.
- Push the crystal at 5 once to the space at 6.
- Pull the lever at 7 once so the beam hits the crystal at 8.
- Pull the lever at 9 twice so the beam hits the crystal now at 6.

This completes the circuit and the beam shoots down to hit the last of the three vault seals, unlocking the vault and spawning a teleport pad nearby.

FIND THE VIAL OF QUICKSILVER

Get ready for some wild combat. Use the teleport pad to a small platform with a key **(20)**. Grab the key and slide down the last chain to the vault platform. Fight your way through many enemies to the locked gate **(21)** and open it with the key. Then fight your way up to the Quicksilver vial and take it to complete the mission.

BACK AT THE RUINS

Watch the Quicksilver bind the magic within the Core of Light. Then listen as the Weapon Master reveals the location of the Eternal Magic Source.

21

ARKEYAN ARMORY

Talk to the Weapon Master and agree to cross the chain to the Arkeyan Armory. When you arrive, he explains that your first task is to restore power to the complex. Unfortunately, doing so will awaken the automated, long-dormant Arkeyan defense forces. The Master says they are formidable, and cannot be deactivated.

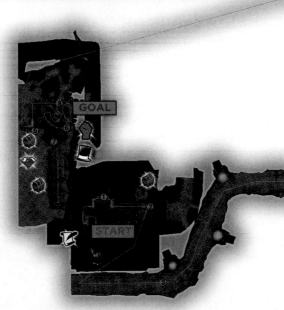

GOAL

START

 Treasure Chest

 Hat

 Soul Gem

 Story Scroll

Legendary Item

—— Direct path from Start to Goal

—— Optional paths for bonus items

OBJECTIVES

USE WAR MACHINE TO FIND TEMPLE

USE SECURITY CARD ON PANEL

USE SWITCHES TO GET THE MAGIC SOURCE

ELEMENTAL GATES

AIR

AREAS TO FIND

UNYIELDING GARRISON

HALLS OF MOLTEN FIRE

THE CRUCIBLE

THE VAULT

PANDORAN GIFT SHOP

NEW ENEMIES

DEFENSE DRONES

CONTROL TOWER

SOUL GEMS

Impervious Tripwire
(Voodood)

LEGENDARY TREASURE

Arkeyan Weapon Controller

HATS

Wizard Hat

STORY SCROLLS

Arkeyan history

Long ago, the evil Arkeyan Sorcerer kings, who lived within dark cities deep underground, met their doom. The Free magicians of Skylands combined their strength to bind the Royal City of Arkus in a vault of eternal sleep. All that remains of their decadent empire are their machines, toiling away in the darkness, for all eternity.

Arkeyan history

MISSION GUIDE

Go down the first ramp and use the yellow-topped switch to restore power. Then use the switch on the opposite side of the landing to roll open the next door. Descend into the first zone, called Unyielding Garrison—no surprise that it's strong in the Tech element. On the way down to the next landing, pick up the Story Scroll entitled "Arkeyan History."

NEW AREA FOUND

"UNYIELDING GARRISON" (TECH)

AWAKEN THE ARMORY

The next landing features your first encounter with the Arkeyan automated defensive grid. Two flying Defense Drones pop out of a spawning pod and open fire. These mini-copters fire projectiles from their wasp-like tails. The most important thing to know is that the ground pod replaces destroyed Drones endlessly unless you destroy the Control Tower, the nearby structure with the green-tipped antenna. Blast the tower, open the next door, and move on.

You can see huge robotic War Machines lined up below as you cross the next platform **(1)**. This area bristles with automated defenses, including two Defense Drone pods with a single Control Tower, surrounded by a ring of Arkeyan Blaster installations. Target the first pair of Blasters from a distance, then push forward and nail the Control Tower next to eliminate the Drone nuisance. Finally, mop up the rest of the Blasters and proceed through the next gate, a force field that dissolves automatically once you eliminate all the defense units.

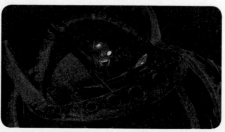

Fight across another Drone-defended platform, then turn left and follow the corridor to a Treasure Chest guarded by Defense Drones. Return and talk to the Weapon Master to learn your next step: pilot the War Machine **(2)** into the inner chamber of the Arkeyan complex. Use the door control to access the loading platform and step into the cockpit of the huge walking War Machine.

PILOT THE WAR MACHINE

The screen switches to first-person view as you look out from the "eyes" (the cockpit) of the War Machine. The great walker starts moving at a steady pace down a long tunnel filled with molten lava **(3)**; you have no control over its speed, and you can only face forward. However, you can swivel the view from side to side by moving the circular targeting reticle.

NEW AREA FOUND
"HALLS OF MOLTEN FIRE"

These Halls of Molten Fire are bristling with defenders. Flocks of Defense Drones zoom at you all along the tunnel, but they inflict little damage on the War Machine so you can largely ignore them. More dangerous are the Ultrons that fire rocket volleys at you from side platforms. Use your primary attack to hammer the Ultrons and/or their platforms with the War Machine's fists. Just move the targeting reticle over each foe and hit your attack button to punch. Try not to miss any Ultrons—if you do, they inflict serious damage as you pass by.

Near the end of the long walk, another War Machine confronts yours **(4)**. The moment you spot it, open fire with the gun activated by your secondary attack button. You can destroy this nemesis before he gets a chance to throw a mega-punch! At the end of the tunnel your Skylander automatically hops out, ready to move on.

Hit the nearby lever to power up the Temple area and get a quick briefing from the Weapon Master: to reach the Eternal Magic Source in the Temple's main vault, you must find a security key card somewhere in the lower level of the Temple and use it on the main security panel **(8)** to deactivate the system. (A quick zoom shows you this panel's location up on the top level.) Once you do this you can flip three switches elsewhere in the Temple to unlock the main vault. When the briefing ends, open the next door and step into a new zone, The Crucible.

NEW AREA FOUND
"THE CRUCIBLE" (AIR)

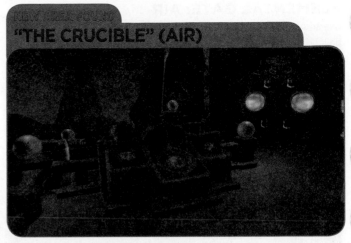

FIND THE SPECIAL ITEMS AND CARD

Fight past squads of Arkeyan Defenders and popup Blaster emplacements until you reach the path split. Take the stairs that head down to the lower level. You can find a number of special items down here. From the bottom of the ramp from the upper level, head down the nearby steps to the beach and spot the legendary item surrounded

by rocks **(5)**. Switch to an Earth Skylander like Prism Break and excavate through the rocks to collect the Arkeyan Weapon Controller.

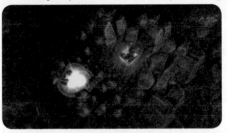

From the rocks, go left and fight through the Defenders to reach a Treasure Chest. Climb the steps back onto the lower level platform and explore the area behind the Temple structure. Fight past the Arkeyan units in the corner and collect the security key card **(6)**.

Further back look for the purple glow of a Soul Gem too. Grab it to unlock the "Impervious Tripwire" power for Voodood. Then, before you take the key card up to the security panel **(8)** at the top of the Temple, check out the elemental gate **(7)** on the beach.

ELEMENTAL GATE: AIR

Use an Air Skylander to unlock the gate and use the whirlwind just beyond to transport past the lava to a big structure in a new area called the Pandoran Gift Shop. (Remember to step quickly out of the whirlwind on the other side or you get sucked right back to where you started.) Climb the staircase to the right to see a series of moving boxes that you can ride across from platform to platform. Note that if you fall off at any time, you can just run to the teleport pad at far left and zap right back up to the structure.

NEW AREA FOUND
"PANDORAN GIFT SHOP" (AIR)

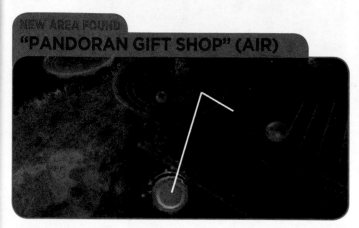

The first two platforms are big and easy to reach. But then you must time your run across three retracting boxes to reach a tiny platform. From there, ride the box toward the camera to find a Treasure Chest. Ride back and continue working your way to the right. Use the bounce pads to get atop the next couple of boxes. Move side to side over the twin rows of moving boxes to reach the hatbox and shake out the powerful Wizard Hat. Then use the teleport pad to get back to the whirlwind exit.

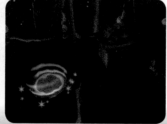

USE THE SECURITY CARD ON THE PANEL

Climb back up to the security panel **(8)** and use the control indicated onscreen to insert the key card. Now go to each of the three vault doors (circled in the overhead screenshot) to throw the switches. Just walk up to the door and it opens automatically. Approach the red switch inside and press the control button displayed onscreen to hit the switch.

NEW AREA FOUND
"THE VAULT"

BACK AT THE RUINS

The Eternal Magic Source completes the Core of Light at last and dispels the Darkness. But the crew doesn't feel safe yet. After all, Kaos destroyed the Core of Light once before. Could he try once again? To end the menace once and for all, General Robot wants to take the fight directly to the enemy's fortress in the Outlands!

Before you head out to the next area, go down to the beach. There's a Winged Sapphire behind the Lock Puzzle. Solve the Lock Puzzle to get the Winged Sapphire.

22
LAIR OF KAOS

Find Hugo over by the railroad tracks on the upper level and talk to him. Agree to enter the portal to the Lair of Kaos. Hugo punches in the coordinates and the Core of Light produces transportation! When you arrive in the dark fortress, Eon offers words of advice, and your destiny awaits.

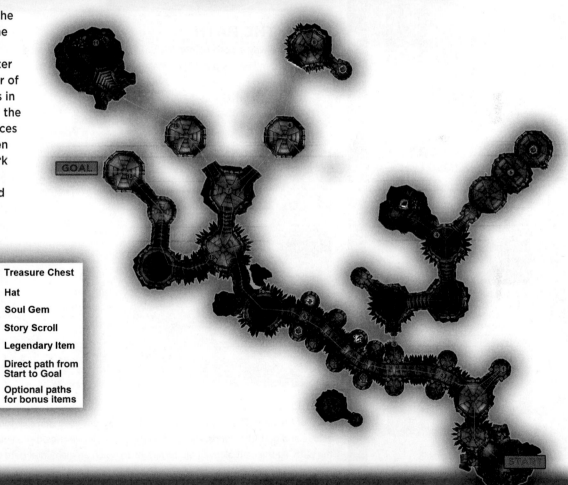

GOAL

🎁 Treasure Chest
🎩 Hat
💎 Soul Gem
📜 Story Scroll
🔷 Legendary Item
—— Direct path from Start to Goal
—— Optional paths for bonus items

START

OBJECTIVES
FIND ENTRANCE TO THE CASTLE

ELEMENTAL GATES
MAGIC

AREAS TO FIND
COLDFIRE CRATER
PATH OF FANGS
TOWERS OF DARKNESS
FORLORN ISLANDS
THE FARTHEST REACH
ALTERNATE ENDS

NEW ENEMIES
NONE

MISSION GUIDE

You start out in Coldfire Crater, strong in the Fire element. The moment you step forward, gaggles of Fire Imps suddenly leap into the clearing to attack. Wipe them out and use the teleport pad to get up onto the first platform. It has a locked gate, and a big Lava King blocks access to the key **(1)**. Drow Witches join him too. Terminate them all, grab the key, and unlock the exit gate.

"COLDFIRE CRATER" (FIRE)

NEW AREA FOUND

COLLECTIONS

SOUL GEMS

*Waterwalker
(Double Trouble)*

LEGENDARY TREASURE

Superior Regalia

HATS

Wabbit Ears

STORY SCROLLS

Origin of Kaos

Some say Kaos was born a prince, but after years of suffering insults about his ugly looks and bad smells, he kicked his father in the widdershins, gave away his royal name and headed out into the wilderness along with his faithful and equally ugly butler, Glumshanks.

Origin of Kaos

WALK THE PATH

The next walkway is aptly named Path of Fangs, strong in the Magic element. Watch out for the huge fangs that line the path! They make painful electric jabs as you pass.

NEW AREA FOUND

"PATH OF FANGS" (MAGIC)

The path features pairs of alcoves, with each pair sitting across from each other on opposite sides of the path. The first pair gives you a choice between gems or food: when you enter one alcove and grab the goods, the gate on the other alcove rises. Take your pick and continue down the path. At the next alcove pair, turn right to reach an elemental gate **(3)**.

ELEMENTAL GATE: MAGIC

Use a Magic Skylander to unlock the gate. Work your way to the right, using bounce pads to hop over the rotating blade platforms. When you reach the path fork, first go left and use the bounce pad to hop all the way up to the hatbox. Shake it open to get the Wabbit Ears. Then go up the other fork **(5)** and use the series of bounce pads to reach the Treasure Chest. Watch out for the impaling spears though! Now return to the Path of Fangs.

FINISH THE PATH

The next alcove pair features some rejuvenating food on one side and a Soul Gem (unlocking the "Waterwalker" power for Double Trouble) on the other. Take your pick—again, you can select only one side or the other. Then use the bounce pad to hop up to the next level of the path. Wipe out the Witches and make another choice, either a gem stash or a Story Scroll entitled "Origin of Kaos."

Continue down the path. The next choice is between gems and food. The last alcove pair **(6)** is a tough decision: a legendary treasure, the Superior Regalia, versus a Treasure Chest. (The item not chosen will be unobtainable until you replay the chapter.)

FIND THREE KEYS

After you make your choice, maneuver carefully around the next rotating blade platform and proceed to the path fork with a triple-locked gate on the left. Obviously, you need three keys to get it open. The first key **(7)** is just up the stairs on the next platform, but you must fight for it.

NEW AREA FOUND
"TOWERS OF DARKNESS" (FIRE)

FIRST ISLAND

With one key in hand, continue up the right fork route into a new zone, Forlorn Islands. When you step to the far side of the platform **(8)** it suddenly detaches and floats off to dock with another island. En route, be sure to stand in the very center of the platform so that the electric fangs don't zap you. When the floater finally docks, KO all of the guards waiting and grab the second key **(9)**. Don't miss the Treasure Chest up in the small attached alcove. Then return to the moving platform, walk to its opposite end to activate it, and ride it back to where you started **(7)**.

NEW AREA FOUND
"FORLORN ISLANDS" (MAGIC)

DIFFERENT PATH ON THE WII

If you're playing Skylanders on the Wii, you get a slightly different look here. Instead of the moving platforms, you must walk down long corridors with claw traps along the way.

SECOND ISLAND

With two keys now in hand, walk to the far side of the other floating platform **(10)**, a new zone called The Farthest Reach. When you step onboard it detaches and floats off to dock with another island. (Remember to stand in the center of the platform.) This one is much more hostile, featuring a quartet of powerful Shadow Knights and a dastardly Tech Spell Punk. Expect a very tough fight, but if you win you can grab the third key **(11)**. Go back onto the floating island to return to the main platform.

NEW AREA FOUND
"THE FARTHEST REACH" (EARTH)

Take your three keys back to the triple-locked gate **(12)** and use them to open it. Fight your way down the path beyond until you reach the last plaza **(13)**, where side platforms keep delivering waves of reinforcements for a last stand, including Drow Witches, Tech Spell Punks, Shadow Knights, and Lava Kings spewing Flame Imps. Wipe them all out! Your victory opens the last gate.

Step through and ride the moving platform over to the castle, where you finally meet the evil master himself, face to face.

DEFEAT KAOS!

Here it is: the final boss battle. It's brutally tough, as these things usually are, so it helps to have a well-developed corps of Skylanders with good stats. In general, you face little that's new: Kaos flings the same nasty minions you've seen in earlier boss battles. Same with the spells cast at you. But in this final confrontation the foes and spells just keep coming and coming!

Kaos' health bar appears on the right side of the screen. Each minion's health bar appears on the left side of the screen as the battle rages. The evil master floats in his throne above the checkerboard grid, then suddenly drops to the ground and summons a minion. He repeats this maneuver again and again. Get in quick hits on the throne before it rises again, then focus on knocking out the minion.

BOSS OF BOSSES

You can't win if you don't take out Kaos himself. So grab every opportunity to punish him when he lets his throne drop to the ground.

After tossing a few minions at you singly, Kaos is done playing games. He summons up the very minion that destroyed the Core of Light and knocked Master Eon into his current spirit-state—the monstrous, four-headed Hydragon! Bad news! Each of its four heads features a special attack. Fortunately, the Hydra heads attack only one at a time.

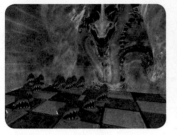 

The blue Water head brings waves of Doom Sharks.

The lava-mouth Fire head summons burning flame spells.

The green Life head hurls explosive, tracking strands of red/green particles. (Remember, the red ones hurt but are also destructible, so hit them from afar to break up the strands.)

And the frightening, skeletal Undead head conjures up a deadly grid of red killer beams.

Again, the good news is that you've seen all of these spells before in earlier boss fights, so you should know what to expect and how best to avoid damage. At certain points Kaos changes things up by introducing new combinations of minions—for example, his "brawlers" the Ice Yeti, Evil Eruptor, and Life Minion, hit you with melee attacks. Later Kaos combines three ranged attackers like his Dark Witch, Pyro Archer, and Amphibious Gillman.

The most important thing to remember throughout the final battles is that it ends only when Kaos' health bar drops to zero. So your very top priority is to blast or whack his throne whenever it drops to the ground.

AFTER THE BATTLE

After you defeat Kaos, watch the amusing finale as the Skylands crew applies an innovative solution to the whiny menace.

ADVENTURE PACK MAPS
EMPIRE OF ICE

(2) ICE MAZE

ICE MAZE

START

GOAL

The Empire of Ice Adventure Pack includes the Empire of Ice bonus Map, the Icicle Isle Battle Mode Arena, the bonus items Sky-Iron Shield and Anvil Rain, as well as the Water Skylander, Slam Bam.

- 🛡 Treasure Chest
- 📘 Hat
- 💎 Soul Gem
- 📜 Story Scroll
- ◈ Legendary Item
- —— Direct path from Start to Goal
- —— Optional paths for bonus items

MAGIC ITEMS

Sky-Iron Shield

Anvil Rain

ADVENTURE PACK MAPS
PIRATE SEAS

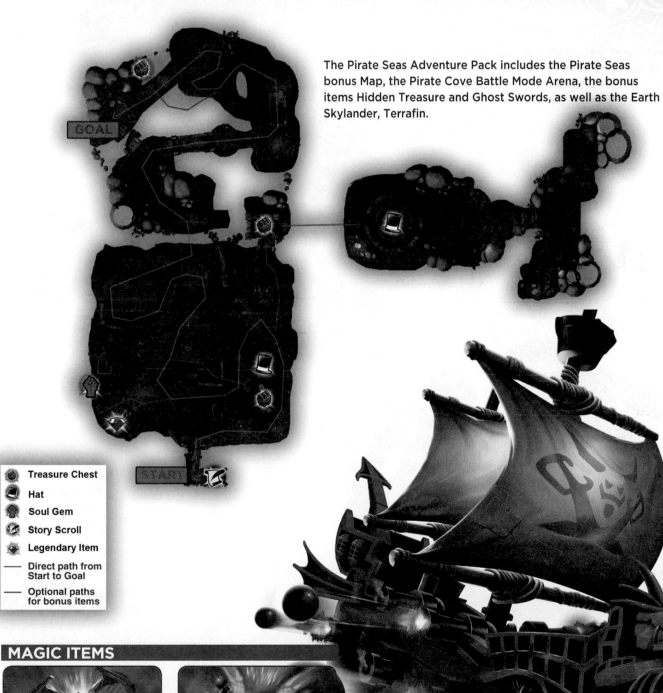

The Pirate Seas Adventure Pack includes the Pirate Seas bonus Map, the Pirate Cove Battle Mode Arena, the bonus items Hidden Treasure and Ghost Swords, as well as the Earth Skylander, Terrafin.

GOAL

START

- 🏺 **Treasure Chest**
- 📖 **Hat**
- 💎 **Soul Gem**
- 📜 **Story Scroll**
- ☀ **Legendary Item**
- —— Direct path from Start to Goal
- —— Optional paths for bonus items

MAGIC ITEMS

Hidden Treasure   *Ghost Swords*

ADVENTURE PACK MAPS
DARKLIGHT CRYPT

The Darklight Crypt Adventure Pack includes the Darklight Crypt bonus Map, The Necropolis Battle Mode Arena, the bonus items Healing Elixir and Time Twister, as well as the Undead Skylander, Ghost Roaster.

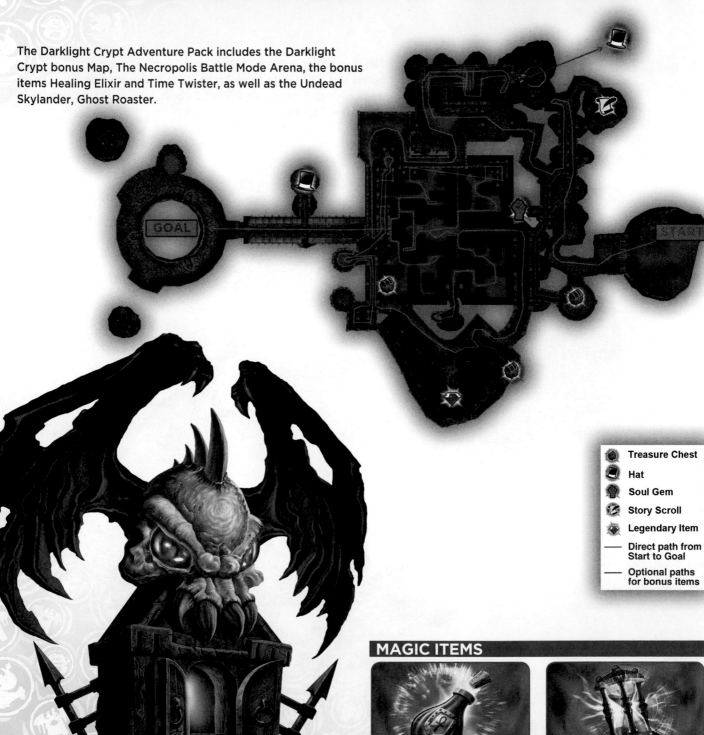

Treasure Chest

Hat

Soul Gem

Story Scroll

Legendary Item

—— Direct path from Start to Goal

—— Optional paths for bonus items

MAGIC ITEMS

Healing Elixir

Time Twister

ADVENTURE PACK MAPS
DRAGON'S PEAK

The Dragon's Peak Adventure Pack includes the Dragon's Peak bonus Map, Cube Dungeon Battle Mode Arena, the bonus items Sparx Dragonfly and Winged Boot, as well as the Fire Skylander, Sunburn.

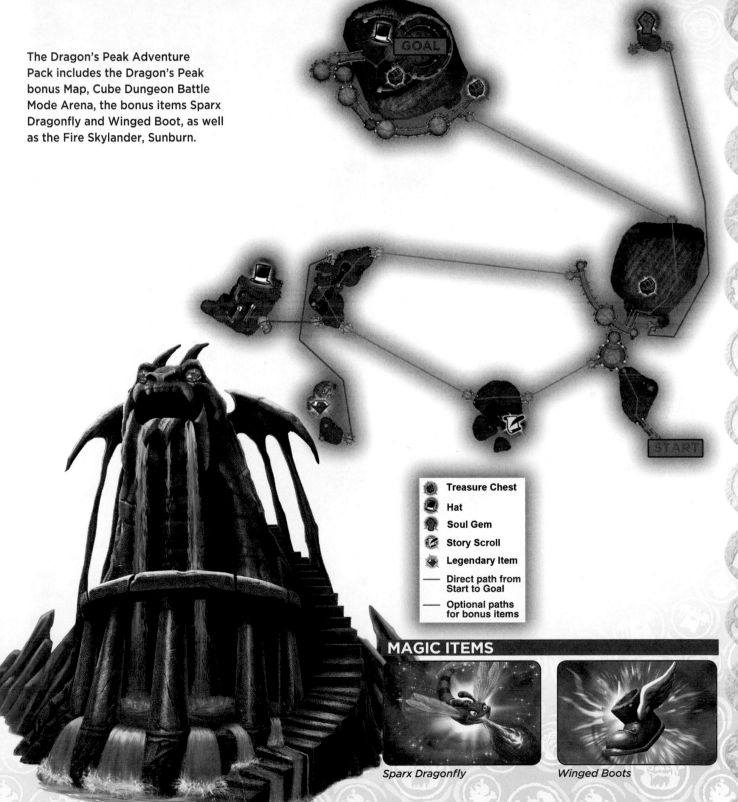

GOAL

START

Treasure Chest

Hat

Soul Gem

Story Scroll

Legendary Item

— Direct path from Start to Goal

— Optional paths for bonus items

MAGIC ITEMS

Sparx Dragonfly

Winged Boots

OFFICIAL STRATEGY GUIDE

By Rick Barba

Please be advised that the ESRB ratings icons, "EC", "E", "E10+", "T", "M", "AO", and "RP" are trademarks owned by the Entertainment Software Association, and may only be used with their permission and authority. For information regarding whether a product has been rated by the ESRB, please visit www.esrb.org. For permission to use the ratings icons, please contact the ESA at esrblicenseinfo@theesa.com.

ISBN 10: 0-7440-1311-9
ISBN 13 EAN: 978-0-7440-1311-5

Printing Code: The rightmost double-digit number is the year of the book's printing; the rightmost single-digit number is the number of the book's printing. For example, 11-1 shows that the first printing of the book occurred in 2011.

14 13 12 11   4 3

Printed in the USA.

Some toys and Adventure Packs sold separately.

BRADYGAMES STAFF

Global Strategy Guide Publisher
Mike Degler

Digital Category Publisher
Brian Saliba

Editor-In-Chief
H. Leigh Davis

Licensing Director
Christian Sumner

Operations Manager
Stacey Beheler

CREDITS

Senior Development Editor
Ken Schmidt

Book Designer
Tim Amhrein

Production Designer
Areva

ACTIVISION CREDITS

BradyGames would like to thank the following people who put in a great deal of time and effort to help shape this guide.

Vanessa Bédard-Lepage
Alex Doherty
Karine Dubé Boies
Jeremy Duvall
Jonny Eco
Vickie Farmer

Rich Hartzell
Elías Jiménez
Peter Kavic
Kevin Kaw
Nick Livingston
Robin Odlum

Misha Sawangwan
Ryan Steiner
Jeff Terra
Karl Von Glahn
Vince Wong